SACRED GARDENS

A Guide to the Traditions, Meaning and Design
of Beautiful and Tranquil Places

MARTIN PALMER & DAVID MANNING

PIATKUS

CONTENTS

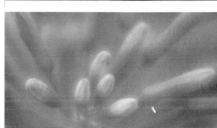
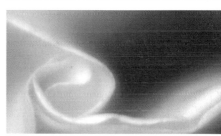
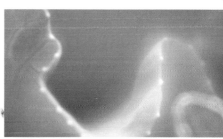

Copyright © 2000 ICOREC

Published in 2000 by
Judy Piatkus (Publishers) Limited
5 Windmill Street
London W1P 1HF
e-mail: info@piatkus.co.uk

For the latest news and information on all our titles,
visit our website at www.piatkus.co.uk

The moral right of the authors has been asserted

A catalogue record for this book is available
from the British Library

ISBN 0 7499 1830 6

Page design by Jerry Goldie
Edited by Lizzie Hutchins
Illustrations by Madeleine David
Botanical consultancy by Dr. Andrew Boorman

Data capture and manipulation by
Create Publishing Services, Midsomer Norton
Printed and bound in Great Britain by
Bath Press (Glasgow) PLC

For many, the creation of a garden, or the care and nurturing of a garden, is of far greater significance than just gardening itself. As I know from my own experience at Highgrove, the garden can become a sanctuary, a place of escape from the noise, rush and often the brutality of the world. It is a place where both humans and wildlife can take sanctuary. The garden in this way can become a glimpse of Paradise; a sacred space where humanity, nature and the Divine meet in harmony.

This is hardly surprising. As this beautiful book so clearly illustrates, the origins of gardening in both East and West are sacred ones. Many of the greatest gardens in history were sacred. We know of the Zen gardens, but I wonder how many of us know about the West's own sacred gardening tradition - of the extent, for example, to which monastic gardens use plants, layout and design to embody spiritual principles? Through this book we can discover something of great importance about our own heritage, as well as be enriched by other spiritual gardening traditions.

In the work of the "Sacred Land" project, run by the Alliance of Religions and Conservation (ARC) and the World Wide Fund for Nature (WWF), sacred gardens play a major role. From the Celtic Christian Meditation garden at Pennant Mellangel, in mid Wales, designed to aid cancer sufferers, to the garden being created at St. Luke's, Barton Hill, in Bristol in memory of the thousands of children who died in the parish during a cholera epidemic in the last century, the creation of such gardens has been the popular choice of communities wishing to embody the sacred in time and space.

This book is not only a practical guide to the creation of a garden as a personal sanctuary, but also an important reminder of the existence of those public "sacred" spaces created in such numbers by the Victorians. The parks, municipal gardens and great cemeteries fashioned during the nineteenth century in so many towns and cities throughout Britain were designed to give ordinary people places of beauty and Nature to rest in. Perhaps we can combine the creation of our own private gardens with a renewed commitment to help create similarly special public spaces in our schools, towns, cities and work places? In this way we can begin to help bring an important aspect of the sacred back into our everyday lives, something our ancestors both understood and valued.

THE IMPORTANCE OF SACRED GARDENS

Legend tells that human life on Earth began in a Garden. Archaeology is uncovering gardens created to bring forth flowers for the deities of ancient Egypt. For the classical Greeks, the wilderness and the sacred forest were places dedicated to spiritual growth. When Jesus wanted to describe Divine glory, he told us to *'consider the lily of the field'*.

For centuries, perhaps for millennia, gardens, trees, flowers – nature itself – has had a central place in spirituality and spirituality has given an especial place to gardens.

It can be argued that the religious history of humanity has repeatedly swung from incorporating nature into the sacred to seeing the sacred incorporated in nature. Today it appears that we have come to understand that both are true at one and the same time. Gardening has never been so popular, nor the spiritual quest so broad. When they combine, the forces unleashed can be extraordinary, profound, beautiful and inspiring. But both gardening and the spiritual quest also entail hard work, proper preparation of the ground, consistency, imagination and endurance.

GARDENS AS SANCTUARIES

The paradise gardens of ancient Persia and Islam (see Chapter 4) were places of refuge from the harshness and barrenness of the desert. Today, for many, gardens fulfil a similar role in contemporary society.

The last hundred years have seen the most wonderful and the most awful actions of humanity. Warfare and violence on an unprecedented scale have contrasted with acts of love, kindness and generosity to rival any other time in history.

In the midst of angst, uncertainty, the crumbling of tradition and all the other features of our changing world, gardens have never been so popular. They have become sacred spaces in which we can leave behind the pressures of an increasingly complex society and find sanctuary, control and personal space.

The desire for gardens is, in part, a revolt against the harsh realities of urban living. For many people, a vital way of putting the immediate demands of our times in a greater, gentler perspective is through the planting of a tree.

This desire to green our lives is perhaps classically expressed in the development of the garden suburb – housing set in landscaped areas. In Britain, the idea of the garden as town was expressed through 'Garden Cities', of which the best known are Welwyn Garden City and Hampstead Garden Suburb. The vision was to create towns in gardens, shrouded by trees and alive with flowers, a million miles away from the treeless, colourless back-to-backs of the 19th century. It was a novel concept and one which, in those places where funds, effort and intention were of the highest level, has worked. But such Garden Cities were too expensive for most local authorities to build and the vast majority of housing developed in the last hundred years allows at best for a small garden plot and at worst for a high-rise flat with few or no redeeming features. It is in the face of this that gardens have come to symbolise a revolt against the brutality of much of the modern built environment as well as against the wars and horrors of the most traumatic century in human history. R. J. Farrer expressed this well in his book *The Rainbow Bridge* in 1918:

> *'The immortality of marbles and of miseries is a vain, small thing compared to the immortality of a flower that blooms and is dead by dusk.'*

Farrer's vision is one shared by many gardeners. It speaks of the sense of being caught up in something beyond us, greater than us and yet of which we are a part. As the world seems to be ever more remote and impersonal, we find sanctuary – and I use that in the true sense of its meaning – in the garden. In many ways, the garden has become the sanctuary.

Nor is it just for us – it is also the sanctuary of many plants and animals, birds and insects. This is well illustrated by just one or two items of the ordinary garden which we take for granted: the bird table and the nesting box. Up until 100 years or so ago, the idea of encouraging wildlife in your garden would have struck most gardeners as very strange. Indeed, many gardeners spent a considerable amount of time and energy tying to keep wild creatures out of their gardens! But now we seek to encourage them through providing nesting boxes, feeding tables shared by birds and squirrels, and food for hedgehogs or in some cases even for foxes.

All this indicates a desire to repopulate the cities and suburbs with the rest of our native creation. We plant buddleias to encourage butterflies because chemical sprays and fertilisers have killed so many of them. We try to support bird populations whose natural habitats have been destroyed in unprecedented numbers. It is as if through our gardens we are trying to undo the destruction of nature which we can see all around us, attempting to turn back the tide of species loss and restore a relationship with nature. As the countryside becomes yet more industrialised and mechanised, so we seek to create a slice of old countryside in our gardens.

> *A garden, even a small one, can stimulate and heal.*

It is significant that one of Britain's best loved gardening writers, Geoff Hamilton, called his last book *Paradise Gardens: Crafting and Planting a Secluded Garden*. In Geoff Hamilton's view, we can manufacture that place so long desired, where the outside world cannot enter in. Through our house walls or walls of trees and hedges, we try to create our walled garden paradise in which we can return to the simplicity of a trusting relationship with nature which was the hallmark of the original Garden of Eden. To people often worn out by the demands of the times, such a garden is as vital as the paradise gardens of Persia on the edge of the ever-threatening desert – a place to retreat to, in order to revive the soul and body.

A garden, even a small one, can stimulate and heal. It can provide hiding-places, secret spaces, a landscape for the imagination of children. *The Secret Garden* by Frances Hodgson Burnett, that wonderful story (and now film) of the healing effect of nature both physical and psychological, on a damaged boy, priggish girl and wounded, mourning father, captures the true magic

of a garden A garden, no matter how small, allows us to enter another world where we encounter nature though our hands, eyes and feet, rather than through our intellect. Even the endless complaint about weeds has an edge of delight. We can bring some order – but we also know it is transient!

Creating a garden is also a way of becoming in tune once more with the cycle of the seasons, a cycle we little notice in our air-conditioned office blocks and homes. In the past, great faiths drew upon the imagery of the seasons to help us understand our place within the greater mystery of creation. Taoism (see Chapter 5) uses the image of the fluctuations of the seasons to illustrate the constant rise and fall of yin and yang. The Book of Ecclesiastes in the Hebrew Bible talks of 'a season for everything' from birth to death.

Gardeners know the reality of the seasons in a way few others do today. The joys and frustrations, possibilities and limitations of every season differ and in that difference lies a profound humbleness before nature. Indeed, many gardeners use the seasons as an almost unconscious meditational tool. In a garden we can feel the joy of spring when life awakens again from a cold, harsh world, when 'dead' branches put forth shoots and leaves, and the softness of soil and colour replaces the harshness of winter. Just think of the glorious carpet of colour in a cluster of bluebells. Nothing humans can construct compares.

In summer we give thanks for the sheer profusion and proliferation of colour, smell, taste and shape, the abundance of flowers and plants, the sense of our gardens being used, by guests, children playing, birds darting to and fro, by animals, bees and butterflies. This outdoor home, as bright and colourful as we can make it, is a place in which to enjoy the warmth of the day and to wander in the cool of the evening.

Autumn then brings intimations of mortality. In a world where the desire for a changeless youth, the fear of old age and the taboo of death are so strong, autumn in the garden allows us to see that decay and death are natural and not to be feared. Autumn is also about taking stock, preparing for hard times ahead, but also planning for new life. It is about tending, protecting and preserving aspects of life often overlooked or dismissed in a world hungry for instant gratification.

Winter offers the time to reflect, to plan for the spring – dreams which usually have to be tempered by time and cost, but are worth dreaming all the same. To see the skeleton of the garden – foliage gone, flowers gone, plants cut back – allows us to appreciate what is permanent and what is transient.

LEFT: Even in the heart of a large city a garden can provide a sanctuary of beauty, tranquillity and spirituality.

Through the year the garden brings us a connection with the changes of the natural world of which we are also a part. And while the seasons fuse gardening and spirituality, so do the actual plants. It comes as quite a surprise to many to discover that the Christian gardeners of the Middle Ages – especially the monks and nuns in the monastic gardens – saw each plant as cosmically significant. Not only do many of the old names indicate direct associations with saints or with Christ, but their astrological importance was also stressed. Plants were seen as part and parcel of a greater pattern, a divine purpose. They were planted not just for their usefulness or beauty, but because they embodied some aspect of God and of the Music of the Spheres.

Likewise, many other ancient cultures saw elements of the cosmos embodied in plants. Greek mythology in particular linked deities, planet and stars with plants. In Vedic tradition, the healing properties of plants were directly related to both astrological and Divine powers.

The gardener is part of something cosmic, a pattern universal, a purpose Divine.

All these notions are stressing the same thing. The gardener is part of something cosmic, a pattern universal, a purpose Divine. It may not feel like it at times when the rain pours down, insects eat flowers and weeds are rampant. But this vision lies behind all the great faith and gardening traditions. In today's world besieged as we are by so many forces of chaos, greed, pettiness and destruction, it is hard to discern this pattern, this purpose. This is why we as gardeners often talk of sanctuaries – just as we who are religious or conservationists also talk of the need to create sanctuaries.

Yet there is also a sense in which our gardens of sanctuary are a kind of retreat – a retreat from the environment around us, the urban landscape. The Georgians and Victorians delighted in planting great rows of trees in the cities and suburbs, in making gardens in town squares, in creating public spaces, in the beautifying of cemeteries. While some of this has continued, not least in the ideals of the Garden City, overall gardening has seen a withdrawal from the public to the private during the last hundred years. In Britain it is hard to immediately think of a major new public park created, say, in the last 50 years. Instead we face a continuing challenge to public open space. School playgrounds are sold off to fund education. Parks are nibbled at by sports centres or shopping malls. The late 19th century–early 20th century vision of a Green Belt around the major cities is under constant attack and loses ground year by year. The end result is the garden as a place of refuge, a sanctuary, rather than a symbol of the brave new public world we might have liked to create.

This phenomenon has led to some significant new developments in sacred gardening. In many cities of the world, it is often only the old religious sites, swallowed up in the growth of great cities, which provide a green space for humans and refuge for wildlife. In Bangkok, for example, Buddhist temples offer welcome relief from pollution and noise for human beings and the last remaining breeding-place for rare birds. In Istanbul, the beautiful ancient mosque and tomb of Eyup, Companion of the Prophet Mohammed, provides, through its vast graveyard, trees and gardens, the last green space on the Golden Horn and the only breeding-place for storks on that formerly beautiful harbour inlet. In the USA, religious communities discover they are guardians of fragments of nature in urban contexts. For example, at St Patrick's Seminar, Menlo Park, California, just south of San Francisco, in a rundown suburb, is the largest remaining wood of native Californian oaks. In Britain, the Living Churchyards Project, a joint venture between churches and conservation bodies, has focused upon the sanctuaries provided by ancient churchyards. Here the land is free of chemicals, and flowers, plants and wildlife, which have been pushed to the margins elsewhere, can find a small home. This is as important in the countryside as in the cities, for the industrialisation of the countryside has been of equal threat to the natural world as the growth of towns.

What we perhaps need to hope for is that the private sanctuary garden is joined by a revival of communal gardening. Allotments are a good example of the fusion of personal and communal. Particularly in industrial cities and towns, they provide a place in which to garden and grow food as well as a communal centre. Side by side, sometimes hundreds, sometimes scores of little plots are tended by their individual owners. But they all belong to a bigger whole, run and organised by the owners themselves. Here communal and private meet and complement each other.

Common ground sites can also produce exciting new schemes. The Sacred Land Project in Europe is working with community groups to create new gardens on derelict land such as dockland sites, old railways lines or the surrounds of ancient religious buildings. Gardens to commemorate the children who died in the great cholera outbreaks of the 1840s are planned in Bristol. In Norfolk, Sikhs are working to create a garden around the tomb of their last Maharajah. In Germany, an old quarry is being turned into a public garden celebrating the diverse beliefs in the community. All these communities are valuing their common past and their need for public gardens to complement the private.

The paradise garden of Geoff Hamilton's dreams is not some vast private estate attached to a palace or grand country home, open to only a favoured few. It is now a possibility for everyone with a patch of land, no matter how small. It can be both our own private garden and a shared public space we choose to make sacred.

For a few, of course, the garden becomes just an extension of their ironed, vacuumed, immaculate front room. Rigid lines and straight borders are perhaps a sign of not being entirely comfortable with the abundance of nature. But most gardens are indeed the place where we meet, share and even contribute to the wonder, glories, triumphs, decay, death and rebirth which is the natural world.

In planning a garden, we unconsciously bring cultural, ascetic, environmental and spiritual assumptions to bear. I enjoy 'translating' gardens for, without realising it, gardeners bare their souls in what they do to and in the garden.

This book offers you the chance to consciously bare or perhaps even find your soul in what you do in your garden. It offers ground plans, models and concepts with which to literally shape your garden. It unlocks the secret language and hidden divinity within plants and flowers. It offers a vision of creativity which joins you to the creativity of Creation and even of the Creator.

And what of sacred gardens in the future? Today we can draw into our gardening an awareness and sympathy not just of our own wonderful traditions of sacred gardening, but also of other religious traditions which former generations either did not have or rather trivialised in fancy pagodas or fake temples. Now we can explore the deeper meaning of a yin/yang garden in our culture. We can see Zen gardens in Western society playing the traditional role they play in Japan. The resources now available are tremendous.

Sacred gardens can mean one of two different things today. They can be a retreat, a sanctuary in which we turn away from whatever else we build and create a reminder of a lost, if romanticised, past. Or they can be a sanctuary from which we go out with a new vision of what could be, harbingers of the way life outside the sacred garden could be lived, celebrated and developed.

To help you understand the potential within sacred gardens, we have designed this book to be a journey in time and place, in faiths and traditions.

We start by taking you back in time to explore the roots of sacred gardening: where, why and how it began. It is a fascinating story of floods and

RIGHT: **Lilium Candidum.** *This flower has traditionally been associated with the Virgin Mary, but is also an important flower in Islamic gardens.*

ice, hopes and fears, and shows us how much which we take for granted, our garden displays and planting schemes, comes as a gift from the peoples of the past.

In Chapters 2 and 3 we enter the world of Christian sacred gardens. In the rush to seek wisdom from the East we can often pass by or ignore the sacred traditions of the West – especially Christianity. Christianity offers an extraordinary array of sacred gardening models and insights, many of which most people in the West are unaware of. Through Gardens of the Life of Christ to Planting Paradise, these chapters open a door to a world many of us have forgotten.

From Chapters 4, 5 and 6 we enter into the sacred worlds and gardens of four major faith traditions. From the Paradise gardens of Islam through the yin and yang based traditions of China to the pebble and sand Zen garden we discover how gardens reveal inner truths and make visible the invisible forces of both nature and the Divine.

Chapters 7 and 8 offer a series of models for those who wish to create a distinctive sacred garden not beholden to any one tradition. The creation of Gardens for Reflection offers new possibilities for the sensitive gardener. Chapter 8 takes this a step further. It shows how the sensory dimensions of a garden can be creatively developed to enhance the spiritual experience.

Finally in Chapter 9 we look beyond the personal garden to those gardens and spaces which are communally owned and over which we can have a much greater impact than many would assume.

This book is a journey and an adventure. It asks you to look at what is familiar and to see the unfamiliar within it. It asks you to explore the land of your garden and the landscape of your soul. It is, we hope, a journey you will make for many years to come.

LEFT: A beautiful garden can become a place for meditation, rejuvenation; even spiritual growth.

1

THE EVOLUTION
OF THE SACRED

For centuries, indeed thousands of years, our ancestors saw gardens as inherently sacred, gifts from God or the gods, bestowed upon humanity. It was our joy and duty to tend and co-create such glorious places. This chapter explores the evolution of the concept of sacred gardens in the West – what the major themes have been, and how they have developed. We also explore the influence of a very different tradition of the sacred in the East.

Central ideas in our understanding of the sacred lie deep within our ancestral memories – they go back to a time of myth and legend – to the dawn of civilisation.

The Withdrawal of the Ice

Until c.13,000 years ago much of the world, especially northern Europe and North America, was in the grip of the last great Ice Age, which lasted over 10,000 years. Over parts of Britain, Scandinavia and Canada the ice was 3,000 m deep (10,000 ft) deep. The ocean levels around the world dropped by around 100 m (330 ft) and the overall temperature of the world fell by about 6°C. On mountain tops in the Middle East, waters and rainfall froze and remained frozen for thousands of years. Ancient rivers dried up because so much water was trapped in the ice. Little grew that was not very hardy.

A NEW WORLD

Probably quite suddenly, the world's climate changed. It used to be assumed that climate changes took centuries, if not millennia, to occur, but this concept has been radically challenged by new evidence. For example, ice core samples from Greenland show that at the end of the last Ice Age the overall temperature of the planet changed by 7°C in just three years.

The effects of the sudden warming of the earth were dramatic in the extreme. As the ice melted, unimaginable quantities of water were released back into the oceans and the air, swelling the seas and combining with rainfall to cause great floods. Ice caps of mountains in the Middle East melted and rivers flowed again. Rainfall increased, bringing forth the ability of the land to produce a wide variety of plants, making it possible for farming and thus gardening to begin.

The garden was an expression of a new relationship with nature and the sacred.

Our ancestors, after perhaps 10,000 years of ice age conditions, found themselves almost overnight – quite probably within a decade – living in a land of unbelievable fecundity, variety and potential. They found themselves in a veritable Garden of Eden. The Bible story does seem to bear witness to a sudden and inexplicable change of fortune.

But it was also a time of threat and terror because of the floods. The sea levels rose by metres every year and land bridges such as those which linked Britain with Europe or Alaska with Siberia, disappeared under the inexorably rising waters. The legends of the flood found not just in the Bible but in so many texts from the Middle East are echoes of the memory of this terrifying time.

By about 12,000 years ago, the world had entered its most recent fruitful period, one which has seen the rise of every known civilisation, of towns, cities and gardens. As nature became kinder to our ancestors, it is possible that the first stirrings of belief in benevolent gods and goddesses also came into being. As nomadic hunters became farmers and settled in villages and towns, perhaps a new and deeper understanding of nature as a face of the Divine emerged. If so – and the Bible and other ancient holy books do indicate this – then one response was to create gardens. It is not too strong a statement to say the creation of the garden was an expression of a new relationship with both nature and the sacred.

EDEN AND PARADISE

Most cultures have their Garden of Eden, their Golden Age, their Age of Perfect Virtue when all was well and everyone lived in balance with nature. In the Bible it is literally the Garden of Eden. In the Abrahamic faiths (Judaism, Christianity and Islam) the story of the Garden of Eden as a sacred space wherein humanity and nature and God co-existed may be a crucial vision of the delicate balance of nature which we inhabit and how sacred such a balance is.

Moreover, such stories ask us to aspire, dream and hope for the best, but also reconcile us to the fact that we rarely if ever find, create or can inhabit such perfect places. They inspire us to strive for more. In a sense, every garden ever planted is an attempt in one way or another to create such places of sacred harmony, always tinged with the knowledge that true harmony lies just beyond our reach.

In the West, sacred gardening has been profoundly affected by two stories, those of the Garden of Eden and of Paradise. Often confused as one and the same thing, these two diverse stories complement each other in a fascinating way. In unravelling them we can discover what each tells us about the nature of the sacred and the sacred in nature.

BELOW: This seventeenth-century depiction of Eden shows the lush fecundity typical of our idyllic view of the original garden.

Judaism and the Garden of Eden

Judaism reveals the Garden of Eden to be the original home of humanity, where God and nature were in a relationship of mutual service. It is a garden whose potential requires the input of human labour and care, guided by God's vision and enabled through the fruitfulness of the Earth. This is perhaps best captured in the following story taken from the Talmud, texts nearly 2,000 years old, which draw out the meaning from the Bible:

> 'Adam walked in the Garden on the first day. He smelled wonderful scents and enjoyed beautiful sights. The aroma of the ripened fruit drew him to the trees. He reached up for an apricot that hung from a branch. The fruit lifted itself so he could not touch it. He reached for a pomegranate. The fruit evaded his hand. Then a Voice spoke, "Till the soil and care for the trees and then you may eat".'

Work was necessary but never onerous and always rewarded. The curse that fell upon humanity as a result of the Fall, when Adam and Eve ate the forbidden fruit and broke that state of collaborative harmony, was not that they have to work itself, but that work would now be hard:

> 'Accursed be the soil because of you.
>
> With suffering shall you get your food from it
> every day of your life.
>
> It shall yield you brambles and thistles,
> and you shall eat wild plants.
>
> With sweat on your brow
> shall you eat your bread...'

(GENESIS 3:17–19)

What was lost in the Garden was that sense of easy living, easy working of the land, which may well have been the actual experience of our forebears as the climate changed after the Ice Age. This was interpreted theologically as a time of blessing but also a time of collaborative work. In Judaism the Fall is understood as the loss of a special relationship with God and nature. Only with the coming of the Messiah is it believed that the original harmony, collaboration, and the Garden of Eden itself, will be restored. Until then, what we experience is but a fallen, dimmed version of the true reality.

The Garden of Eden as understood by Judaism echoes the experience of the brief period when the Middle East was awash with river waters and highly fertile. This probably lasted from c.13,000 to maybe 8,000 years ago.

Then the climate changes went too far the other way. The ice caps had melted and the sun now parched lands which for a while had been moist and well watered. Eden had turned out to be a brief and passing experience. Thereafter it was the sweat of one's brow which brought forth fruit.

Christianity and the Garden of Eden

Christianity inherited the Jewish vision and began to rework it. Some traditions retained the notion of Adam and Eve working in the garden – echoed in the Christian Socialist cry of 'When Adam delved and Eve span, who was then the gentleman?' – but for many Christians Eden was a state of divinely sanctioned laziness, with everything provided and nothing required except obedience. This is why the disobedience of Adam and Eve has become so central to the Christian understanding of the significance of the Garden and why the notion of Original Sin was created. In Judaism, the Fall is the loss of a fruitful partnership leading to a life being a greater struggle. In Christianity the Fall becomes a great chasm between God's demands for obedience and humanity's foolishness in disobeying. What both faiths share is the use of the term 'garden' to describe the primal, original and harmonious state

Gardens are an attempt to create harmony between God, humanity and nature.

of not just human, but also humanity and nature under the benevolent Eye of God. Again, we can see why gardens in the West have been for so long an attempt to create in miniature the perfect balanced harmony of God, humanity and nature. It is perhaps Judaism's special wisdom to have always known that to create such a balanced harmony, humanity had to work to make its contribution.

The Origins of Paradise

The term 'Paradise' does not occur in Jewish texts of the Bible. It was introduced by Greek scholars who translated the Hebrew Bible into Greek in the 2nd century BC. And the Greeks got the word from the ancient religious language of Persia, the Zend, which is where the word originates. Paradise – in Greek *paradeisos* – comes from the Zend word *pairidaeza*, meaning a walled pleasure garden designed to offering shade, beauty and a place for contemplative strolls or liaisons.

Classically, this was a prince's garden, designed for comfort and beauty in the midst of hot cities or on the edge of desert plains. Unlike the Jewish story of the equality of the labourer with the user of the garden, Persian *pairidaeza* were probably created by slaves and used by the aristocracy who didn't even think of the labour involved.

It is possible that the concept of the paradise garden evolved from more ancient Near Eastern and even Egyptian influences. The Hanging Gardens of Babylon in many ways seems to embody the concept of Paradise with its terraces, fountains and exotic flowers and plants.

In Egypt the fertility of the land was a cause for celebration, expressed through the ancient Egyptians' love of nature and, in particular, flowers and plants. It was not unusual for guests at a banquet to offer each other sweet-scented lilies as wine might be offered now. The deities were adorned with garlands and the capitals of the temple columns were carved in the shape of lotus flowers or papyrus buds. Flowers, herbs, vines, fruit and vegetables were cultivated for the home and for votive offerings. For the many Egyptians who had sufficient land and money to cultivate one, the private garden was also a much loved place of pleasure and tranquillity, but gardens were also very important to the priesthood and walled gardens were attached to temple complexes.

THE HANGING GARDENS OF BABYLON

Perhaps the most famous of ancient gardens are the fabled Hanging Gardens of Babylon, built by Nebuchadnezzar II (604–562 BC) for his wife. Greek writers provide our only knowledge of these gardens. One of the best descriptions is as follows:

The Garden is quadrangular – it consists of arched vaults which are located on checquered cube-like foundations. The ascent of the uppermost terrace-roofs is made by a stairway… The Hanging Garden has plants cultivated above ground level, and the roots of the trees are embedded in an upper terrace rather than in the earth. The whole mass is supported on stone columns… Streams of water emerging from elevated sources flow down sloping channels. These waters irrigate the whole garden, saturating the roots of plants and keeping the whole area moist. Hence the grass is permanently green and the leaves of trees grow firmly attached to supple branches… this is a work of art of royal luxury and its most striking feature is that the labour of cultivation is suspended above the heads of the spectators.

ABOVE: This etching by William Walcot shows a 20th century interpretation of the Hanging Gardens of Babylon.

The Christian Concept of Paradise

Whatever its ancient antecedents it is clear that by the time of the New Testament, Paradise had come to mean a state of being in the future – part of the Second Coming of Jesus, for example. Thus in Luke 23:43 Jesus upon the cross turns to the repentant thief and says: 'Indeed I promise you today you will be with me in Paradise.'

Greek and Russian Orthodox iconography usually shows Paradise as a classic Persian garden, walled, beautifully planted with trees bearing fruit, a lawn of radiant flowers and bright green grass and water flowing through it along channels dividing the lawns. It is a future state of perfect contentment, where the inhabitants receive their reward for a good life on Earth, the epilogue to balance the prologue of the Garden of Eden in the great cosmic story of God, humanity and creation.

In Islam, the Paradise model was taken even further. For Muslims, Paradise is where we all dwelt before the Fall and it is where we shall return to if we die as believers. It is a perfect world where no labour is. The interesting thing here is that Paradise is not on this world – it is another planet altogether. The Fall was literally a fall from this perfect planet to the Earth, where we have to work through the consequences of the human rebellion which led to our being expelled before we can return. This is clearly set out in this text from the Qur'an:

We said:

'O Adam, dwell thou and thy wife in Paradise; and eat of the bountiful things therein as (where and when) ye will, but approach not this tree, or ye run into harm and transgression.'

Then Satan made them slip from Paradise and got them out of the state of felicity in which they had been. We said: 'Get you down, all you people, with enmity between yourselves. On Earth will be your dwelling place and your means of livelihood – for a time.'

(SURAH II:35 36)

This story reflects a later set of traditions and the impact of an environment where water is precious. Memory of the garden state after the Ice Age seems to have faded significantly. Instead we hear a story of Paradise which comes from a culture of gardening. Paradise is a created garden, one which in its very formality shows that it has been wrought out of desert and wilderness. It is a haven in an environment which is now generally unfriendly.

The mythology of Eden and Paradise has been the defining mindset and way of seeing nature for the West for over 2,000 years. Until the 15th century gardens were laid out largely according to sacred geometry shaped by Eden and Paradise. For example monastic gardens embody many aspects of both Eden and Paradise in their emphasis on productive nature as well as the enjoyment of beauty for its own sake. Monasteries contained herb gardens, for both culinary and medicinal purposes, vegetable gardens, but also areas for meditation and reflection. Chapter 2 is devoted to exploring in detail every aspect of the monastic garden while Chapter 4 explores more fully the concept of Paradise embodied in the Islamic garden.

However, while the Abrahamic traditions focused on the concept of nature as a garden, the classical world provided a different model: a model that, although forgotten for centuries, was to be revived in the West in the early modern period and remains important to this day.

THE SACRED GROVE

The sacred grove was a very different kind of garden and one whose influence on gardening in the West has been seriously underestimated. The sacred grove was the wilderness tamed yet kept with an element of wildness. In Greece sacred groves were often fragmentary remains of ancient forests, the rest having been destroyed for fuel, building or land clearance.

In the sacred grove, we can see a romantic attachment to the lost wild forest, home of feared deities and wild animals, even perhaps of the spirit of nature which was recognised and often feared in women. The groves were manageable but frightening; dark enough for the Mysteries to be performed in heavily forested parts or caves, yet small enough to not prove a real danger. The ancient Greeks' sacred groves were often dedicated to Diana, the goddess of hunting.

Sacred groves are found in many ancient civilisations. In India they still exist and indeed have recently had a new lease of life. The sacred groves of Krishna, surrounding his birthplace in Vrindavan, north India, have been worshipped for centuries, perhaps millennia. In recent years they have become deforested through abuse, forgetfulness, neglect and population pressure. Today, however, they are being restored and enlarged as part of a wider environmental awareness programme of the Hindus.

NEW CONCEPTS IN SACRED GARDENING

In the West the concept of celebrating untamed nature was largely forgotten until the 18th century. It is not until the early modern era that new ways of looking at nature and gardening emerged. One reflected the Reformation and the development of a scientific approach to the world which sees God

ABOVE: *This painting by the Master of Oberrheinischer shows a medieval view of a walled Paradise garden featuring irises, Madonna lilies, strawberries, roses and lily of the valley.*

as the divine watchmaker of a rational natural order. The other was in many ways a revival of the ancient Greek concept of the sacred grove: a new appreciation of nature wild and pristine. These two impulses have fluctuated in their popularity until the present day.

From Sacred Gardener to Sacred Watchmaker

By the 16th century the understanding of sacredness had changed in much of the Protestant Western world. Gone was the medieval concept of a mystical God the Father who worked through miracles and priests in a sacramental way and instead the God of early science came into being — the rationalistic God who, like a watchmaker, sets the world running along prescribed lines but does not intervene through incarnations, miracles or other such manifestations. To a certain degree, the sacred was now more of a formula, devoid of the unexpected, stripped of the supporting ranks of angels and cleared of all that seemed to suggest disorder or unpredictability. Instead the world was rational and reasonable. God created this order and was bound by

it. Gardens needed to reflect this.

Furthermore, the Reformation gave people the sense that they could talk to God, 'face to face'. There was no need for intermediaries. Thus the garden, especially the sacred in the garden, moved away from symbol to a sense that in the garden humanity and God met almost as equals.

To look on a small garden such as that of Little Moreton Hall in Cheshire, England, dating from the late 16th century, is to see the order of the new theology. With its exquisite knot garden and quartered garden, all of which can be viewed from a small man-made hill, we see everything in its place and everything having a place; pattern and order repeating itself endlessly, all controlled from the view on the hill. God observes from afar that all is in order – as the owners of Little Moreton Hall could observe their own kingdom.

By the early 18th century, all formal European gardens were exactly that – formal spaces laid out to reflect the symmetry and precision of the laws of the order of the universe and of God.

This has remained a powerful tradition in gardening. The concept of humanity's ability to rationally control nature was also, for example, important to the Victorians. As Victorians enjoyed the fruits of the Industrial Revolution and the Empire, there was a sense of being blessed by God as science and technology improved the world. As one hymn writer summarised it optimistically: 'God is working His purpose out, as year succeeds to year.'

Nineteenth-century European horticulturists set out to improve gardens armed with the latest discoveries and technologies. They imported vast numbers of new species to add a brilliant lustre and shine to their gardens with dazzling flowers such as marigolds, heliotrope, geraniums and lobelia, or with bushes such as the rhododendron. They invented the lawn mower (first patented in 1832), which meant smooth lawns could be sustained without the need for grazing sheep; they perfected hot houses where nature could be 'brought on'. Many saw themselves as partners with God in spreading the beauties and wonders of his creation. Indeed, one can go further and say that they saw themselves as co-creators with God.

The rationalist view of nature, however, always contained within it the seeds of the opposite view. For the 18th-century romantics a delight in the artificial 'wilderness' arose in reaction to the rigidity of the formal garden. As the 18th century became the 19th humanity's relationship with nature became more ambiguous and problematic still. The Industrial Revolution brought with it huge migration to the cities and a growing sense of alienation from the land. At the same time as the Victorians celebrated their ability

LEFT: *The knot garden at Barnsley House, Gloucestershire, a perfect example of order imposed upon chaos.*

to order and control nature, they desperately began to seek out nature wild and untamed in the Romantic passion for rambling and the beginnings of conservation movements to protect areas of wilderness.

It is at this point that the natural garden emerges most fully as a new approach to gardening and the sacred. This concept had ancient antecedents; as we have seen in the sacred groves of the Greeks, but also in the view of nature of a completely foreign culture: the Chinese.

THE NATURAL GARDEN

Until the 17th century China was virtually unknown in the West. Then, from the early 17th century until the end of the 18th century, European Jesuits held highly honoured positions in the Chinese imperial court and from this vantage point reported back to an incredulous yet dazzled Europe.

While the Jesuits had great respect for many aspects of Chinese culture, they seemed to find it impossible to understand Chinese gardens. Louis le Comte, writing in his *Journey through the Empire of China* (1699) noted:

> *The Chinese so little apply themselves to order their Gardens, and give them real Ornaments, do yet delight in them, and are at some cost about them: they make grotto's in them, raise pretty little Artificial Eminences, transport thither by pieces whole Rocks, which they heap one upon another, without further design, than to imitate Nature.*

To the Western mind, nothing could have been further from their idea of a true garden than such apparent lack of order. The Chinese understanding of nature, which is that it has its own way, its Tao, which we are part of and that we need to be part of fully, was also totally foreign. Yet slowly the idea of a garden which was natural, which celebrated the uncertainties of mountain streams and sought the irregularity of rocks and woods, began to seep into Western thought.

It is perhaps difficult for us to appreciate that until the very end of the 17th century, few people saw anything worth commenting upon in nature. Indeed, to many it was frightening, alien. But with the 'discovery' of nature and landscape, aided by the rise of the Romantic poets who expressed in verse the love of wilderness as a counterpoint to the spreading cities and

ABOVE: Stourhead in Wiltshire, England, where meticulous landscaping is used to create a 'natural' garden.

the rise of industrialisation, things changed radically.

From the late 18th century delight in artificial 'wildernesses', most famously created by the landscape gardener Capability Brown, transformed into a kind of urgency to protect and emulate pristine nature. Throughout the 19th century the first national parks specifically designed to protect areas of wilderness appeared in the United States, while in Britain existing areas of heath and commons were protected as cities rapidly expanded. For example it was at this time that areas such as Hampstead Heath in London were protected as public space.

This emphasis on public space is interesting, for the Victorian appreciation of the 'natural' garden occurred not so much in private gardens, but in the development of a new concept – urban parks. This in turn heralded a new stage in sacred gardening.

Urban Parks

Urban parks have their origins in England with the royal parks. St. James's Park, London, for example, was opened to the public in the mid 17th century. 'Pleasure gardens' – essentially entertainment gardens where you paid to enter – originated around the same time. The most famous were Vauxhall Gardens, London, begun in 1661 and finally closed in 1859, by which time 'pleasure' had acquired a rather unsavoury and dubious reputation!

In creating the public parks, the Victorians and their imitators in America and Europe sought to alleviate the horrors of urbanisation through a deliberate creation of a rural idyll, a wooded retreat or a series of country walks, capturing, in the midst of industrial development unparalleled anywhere before, a vision of 'nature' which harked back to the great parks of the 18th century yet incorporated the bedding plants and colourful profusion of the 19th-century 'gardenesque' movement (the improvement of nature through human skills). Many of the great public parks incorporated 'natural' areas; for example Battersea Park, in London, has its own 'wilderness' garden.

What is so dramatic and innovative about the Victorian great gardens is that they were not just for the wealthy. It is perhaps important to recall that until the 19th century, no one had built great parks and gardens explicitly for the ordinary people. Eden had come home and was being built amidst the black nightmares of Cain's efforts – for the Bible says that after murdering Abel, Cain built the first city.

There is truly a redemptive aspect to the public parks of the 19th century which is as much to do with spiritual redemption as it is to do with good health. They were creating sacred space for new communities, drawing upon a sense of balancing human activity with a place of rest which reflects Genesis 1, where on the seventh day, God rested and walked in the garden. The Biblical command to rest on the seventh day had to be enforced by social reformers, because mill owners tried to make their workers labour seven days a week. As part of the struggle, led by Christians, for a day of rest, there needed to be places to rest and relax in. Hence the need for public parks – part of the restoration of the Divine model for life.

THE ARBORETUM

The first public park, designed as such and as a contrast to the industrial growth around it, was the Arboretum in Derby, England, opened in 1840. This philanthropic venture was the result of the benevolence of Joseph Strutt, whose mills dominated the nearby town of Belper, and the designs of the extraordinary John Claudius Loudon. He was the main moving force behind what is referred to as the 'gardenesque' movement. He founded the first regular journal for gardening enthusiasts, *The Gardener's Magazine*, which was immensely influential for much of the 19th century. The tremendous public response to the Arboretum showed how popular such places were. Writers were entranced by the creation of 'renewed nature' amidst the houses. When Strutt opened the Arboretum, he compared the work done by Loudon in creating the park with the social reforms also taking place at that time. The public garden was more than just a pretty space. It was a reform. Such parks were trying to put a sense of natural religion back into violated environments.

SACRED GARDENS TODAY

Today our concept of the sacred incorporates all of these traditions: the conservation movement and the influence of Eastern philosophy has heightened our awareness of the beauty of the untouched natural world and many gardeners try to create their own wilderness through informal plantings and encouraging wildlife into the garden. For others order in the garden represents a sacred harmony between man and the Divine – an indication that humans can have a fruitful and productive partnership with the natural world.

In the midst of these often contradictory impulses and influences the concept of Eden and Paradise seems to remain a potent description of our understanding of sacred gardening. As gardeners we need to keep a balance between Eden and Paradise. Eden shows us that this world can provide a near perfect environment to dwell in and that human activity can enhance or destroy it. It emphasises the sacred nature of what we have been given. For many in the world today, the garden is indeed fruitful. We, however, must 'tend and care', as Adam was told.

Paradise shows us that even in the depth of urban chaos, environmental destruction or wilful neglect, it is possible to create something which gives a taste of Heaven. So, when Eden has been destroyed, lost or forgotten, we can still create a Paradise garden. Gardening is a sign of hope. It tries to create beauty out of disorder and meaning out of what lies around us. As such it is as sacred an activity as prayer or liturgy, or the construction of great cathedrals or magnificent temples. It is a hint of what has been and a foretaste of what could be to come – both Eden and Paradise.

ABOVE: Even the smallest garden can become a sacred space.

2

THE MONASTIC GARDEN

In the early 8th century, the great and saintly monk, Alcuin, wrote from his homeland in northern England to Charlemagne, King of the Franks. Alcuin tells the great king how he has worked to bring the beautiful flowers of Britain into France. He writes of his hope that the French may learn the wonders of gardening from the British, so that a paradise – a 'garden enclosed' – may flourish not just in York, but also in Tours, and that there might be 'the plants of paradise with the fruits of the orchard'.

Gardens and Christianity were two of the greatest legacies Rome gave to Britain. But they did so in the midst of a mini eco-crisis brought about by the ruinous practices of late Roman agribusiness. Essentially, the collapse of urban Roman civilisation in the 4th to 6th centuries AD, in much of France, the Rhineland and at the least southern Britain, was largely the result of the collapse of the local agriculture.

It may be hard for us to believe now, but the lands of northern Egypt were once the richest wheat fields of the Roman Empire. This now desolate area originally provided all the grain necessary to feed the whole city of Rome and its surrounding towns. Through Roman over-exploitation, this rich farmland became the desert it is today.

THE MONASTIC HAVEN

In northern Europe, a very similar pattern emerged. Big business bought up the original small land holdings and created vast estates, run as aggressively as any major agribusiness today. By the end of the 5th century AD, much of modern-day France, Belgium, southern Germany and England was a waste land of over-exploited soil and lost tree cover. It was into this destruction that Christianity brought healing of the land and of nature through the farming and gardening techniques developed especially by the Benedictine monastic order, founded in AD 515.

The rise of monastic Christianity was a reaction against Roman, urban Christianity. It led to the restoration of agriculture and horticulture, which created the farms, gardens and beauty of so much of northern Europe in the centuries after Rome and whose passing through the changes in agriculture today we so mourn. The rolling green hills and fields, orchards, streams full of fresh water, the village ponds, gardens, herbs and flowers for our use – all and more of this beauty we owe to the pioneering, loving and Godly work of the monks and nuns. They not only developed best practice in woodland management, drainage, soil enrichment, fertilisers, orchards, vineyards, pleasure gardens and herbal gardens, but they also wrote much of it down and helped preserve the wisdom of the classical writers on plants. Medicine – virtually all of it herbal – was a major factor of every monastery and required intimate knowledge of the properties of plants and flowers.

Christian architecture has long celebrated nature through its carvings, stained glass and misericords. For example, the Chapter House at Southwell Cathedral in Nottinghamshire, England, provides one of the most important visual records of common plants of the early Middle Ages. Carved on every corbel, arch and capital is a mass of plants and flowers, accurate in every detail.

The essence of the monastic garden is a Christian fusion between place and space, plants and symbolism, usefulness and beauty, all caught up in a vision of nature, humanity and God as being in a unity of purpose and intention. By careful design and by bringing the meditative qualities of monastic insights to bear, we can re-create something of this. Let us look at these component parts.

Place and Space

Chinese *feng shui*, or geomancy, has become very popular in the West because of the way in which Chinese buildings, landscape and garden design are aligned with directions and with spiritual forces. In the West we seem to have forgotten our own Christian geomancy. Our churches, shrines, holy wells, sacred mountains and even towns and cities were laid out to reflect a belief that they represented a microcosm of the universe. Most people know that churches face East. But why? Because East is the direction of the cosmically significant Jerusalem and the direction of the rising sun, an ancient symbol for the Resurrection of Christ. Most of us know this, yet never give it the significance it deserves.

Orientation of a site towards a sacred direction is as old as sacred sites in the land. Many burial mounds, stone circles, churches and mosques point towards a sacred direction associated with the sun, moon, a landscape feature, a holy place or site. They focus us upon the purpose of the building or site and link us with untold millions throughout the world and through history who have also focused us on the same sacred place.

Plants and Symbols

Creating a space for reflection is part and parcel of all sacred gardens. In a garden, this can again be in the East. In one garden I saw long ago, the East was dominated by a magnificent hawthorn tree. This stark and tough tree drew your eye, a symbol of death and pain but which also bursts into flower shortly after Easter.

Creating a space for reflection is part and parcel of all sacred gardens.

Such symbolic use of plants and trees lies deep within the traditions of Christian sacred gardens. The monks and nuns of old saw all plants as having a symbolic significance, reflected in the names linking them to saints, angels or to healing – a Christian vocation blessed by Christ's own healing ministry. Think of the vast number of plants which bear the names of saints, such as perforate St. John's wort (*Hypericum perforatum*), which flowers on St. John's feast day, midsummer, and whose patterning looks like the wounds he suffered. The British Isles even has plants associated with the Holy Trinity, as for example the association St. Patrick made between the three sections of a clover leaf and the Trinity – like the Trinity all three sections are equal, distinct but linked and thus forming one.

It may also surprise you to discover that the astrological significance of plants was taken very seriously by Christians in the Middle Ages, especially by monks. The belief that all life had its ruling planets was taken for granted. For example, harebell, *Campanula rotundifolia*, traditionally has Venus as its ruling planet and so is associated with reducing bleeding, not least during menstruation. The monks and nuns took very seriously the ruling planets of each plant, for they saw their work in gardening and landscaping as creating the cosmos in miniature, and the stars and planets were an essential part of this. It is only when we can learn to see such work as cosmic, and as reflecting the total interrelationship between all that God has made, that we can begin to understand the power and significance of such monastic gardens.

Utility and Beauty

Herbs have both a functional use and a symbolic use. The healing herbs, such as those described on pages 44-45, should be cultivated with due care

to their powers. The monastery 'herb gardens' reflect the concern for physical healing which has always been a hallmark of Christianity. Almost all the great hospitals of Europe, and many in North America and Australia, owe their origins to Christian monasteries, and healing continues to be a major part of the life of many churches. The healing herbs of the monastery garden are a practical expression of this vision.

The enjoyment of all that God provides has been a constant theme in Christian prayer and life. Fasting and feasting are still of tremendous significance in the Christian world and herbs which draw out or complement the flavours of different meats or vegetables, play an important part. The heart of the Christian life is a shared meal: the communion. In Christian belief, every meal is a potential communion and should be shared with all. The visitor, traveller or the homeless were welcomed and fed at the monastery for a maximum of three days without question.

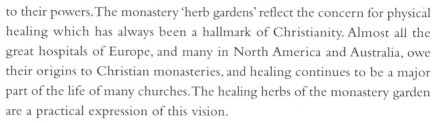

BELOW: The Cloisters Garden in New York. These 12th century transplanted cloisters are planted with shrubs, trees and flowers typical of medieval European gardens.

THE MONASTIC LANDSCAPE

Central to not just the layout of the gardens but also to the design of the whole monastery is the idea that buildings should be in cosmic harmony with their environment and landscape. Accordingly, the plan of a monastery was determined by the 'geomantic' orientation of the church itself, which faced East. The gardens to the East, behind the altar and great East windows, were designated as 'Paradise' gardens. To this day it is still common to find, in even ordinary ancient parish churches, that the graves, footpaths and ordered planting is on the South, West and North sides, though the flower garden lies to the East, and that the area to the East, though perhaps including an orchard cemetery, generally has fewer graves and looks more 'natural', as if capturing something of the lost Garden of Eden, or suggesting the natural state of Paradise.

Imagine seeing the monastery as the monk planners saw it. At its heart, symbolically sacredly aligned, lies the church, a living cross shape, in stone, glass, paint and worship, alive with colour from statues, frescoes and mosaics, a thing of beauty in adoration of God. Surrounding this, again in symbolically sacredly aligned places, are flowers, trees and bushes, reflecting and complementing the beauty of the painted carved church. Sweet scents from blossom, the irregularity of trees, the openness and freshness of greenery, the vibrancy of flowers all made a glorious complementary harmony, a microcosm of Heaven, of Paradise, of life as it could be.

Meditative Areas

The rest of a classic monastic landscape seems to be based on a mixture of Roman villa design, overlaid with a highly practical and contemplative Christian interpretation. Thus one feature still to be seen at almost any ancient monastery – or in any of the cathedrals which were once monasteries – is the cloister garth. This is usually a beautifully kept lawn or turf around which, through the cloisters, monks walked in meditative reflective procession at regular intervals each day. The garth is laid out in a formal way, usually subdivided into four quarters by pathways similar in appearance to Roman villa gardens. Some people also see an Islamic paradise influence here. Water was often present and the monks could reflect on the key elements of water, earth, sky, air and rock. The cloisters around the lawn meant that much of the hustle and bustle of life within and beyond the monastery was kept out. To this day, even in the busiest of city centres, an old cloister garth is an oasis of peace and calm.

In a sense, the emptiness and regulated order of the cloister stresses the space at the heart of contemplation. The great mystics – St. John of the Cross, Mother Julian – knew that beyond words, beyond images, beyond the expressible lies the utter otherness of God. In the presence of God, all is inadequate. The empty cloister garth thus perfectly captures the Divine Space, Divine Emptiness at the heart of nature and of contemplation. Even the hurrying visitor today who wanders into the garths of Wells Cathedral, Somerset, England, the National Cathedral, Washington D.C., USA, or the Basilica of St. Francis, Assisi, Italy, can still find that peace which, as the Book of Common Prayer (1662) of the Church of England puts it, 'passeth all understanding'.

THE MONASTIC DESIGN

A template for the classic monastic garden layout was provided by the famous and slightly idealised plan of the monastery of St. Gall, Switzerland. The gardens at St. Gall so inspired the Emperor Charlemagne (AD 742–814) that he ordered every city in his empire (which consisted of western Germany, France and the Italian Alps) to plant a herb garden. His edict to do so contained a helpful list of plants and this, one of the earliest documents on gardening to survive, is known as the *Capitulare de Villis*. It became a standard text throughout Continental Europe.

The Orchard Cemetery

Another place of contemplation, and usually placed to the East end, is the orchard cemetery. This utilitarian approach might come as a surprise to a more squeamish generation, but in the Christian life, death is but a gateway to a greater glory. The body falls away and Heaven opens to the believer. Heaven itself was pictured as a garden and thus the idea of fruit trees and bones would have presented no problems to the monks.

The Flower Garden

Also in the sacred eastern direction lay the flower garden. This was the sacristan's garden. The sacristan was the monk in charge of the sacred objects, and thus also of the decoration of places such as the high altar. In his garden he grew flowers for decoration and for beauty.

The Herb Garden

Elsewhere, often to the North of the eastern end, but sometimes in the cloisters or courtyards beside the church, lay the herb gardens. There were two main types of such gardens. The first was the infirmary or physic garden. This was quite a large area, divided by pathways creating a series of raised beds, perhaps as many as 16. Each bed was used for a different medicinal herb, for to use the wrong plant could cause illness or even death.

The second major herbal garden was the kitchen garden, where, besides vegetables, there would be culinary herbs such as mint, thyme and parsley.

Other Areas

'The green court' is a term used to describe the use of open space between the more dispersed ancillary buildings, such as bakeries, storerooms, etc. This area would be open grass or pasture with trees and perhaps the occasional bush or hedgerow.

'Obedientiary gardens' were the private gardens of the abbot and other important figures in the monastery. These gardens resembled the gardens of the nobility with trellised courtyards resplendent with roses, honeysuckle and other climbers. The monastic notables might have sat with their guests on the turf seats — so distinctive in paintings of the Middle Ages.

CREATING A MEDICINAL HERB GARDEN

A Christian herb garden can be created in the garden or in the house. Much of the basic information necessary is of course common to both. Let us assume you want to create a medicinal herb garden.

Some useful herbs for your garden include dill (*Anethum graveolens*), with its beautiful feathery leaves. The seeds and leaves can be used to make a rather sharp drink which aids relaxation and assists the digestion – this is a plant to use for meditation perhaps, when the body is tense and needs a natural way to relax.

If you suffer from nerves or tend to get very anxious, then judicious use of valerian (*Valeriana officinalis*) can also help you relax. The dried roots or the juice can be used to prepare a drink.

The beautiful flowers of the clove-pink (*Dianthus caryophyllus*) make a delightful show in the garden, but also produce a tincture which is used to soothe headaches and other signs of tension and anxiety.

The umbrella flowers of the fennel (*Foeniculum vulgare*), with their distinctive yellow colour, make a good tea or can be added to salads. Both the seeds and leaves can be used to calm upset stomachs, especially if the upset

TRADITIONAL MONASTIC HERBS

KEY
s = sun p.sh = partial shade
sh = shade

CHIVES (*Allium schoenoprasum*)
Hardy perennial; s/p.sh. Height up to 60 cm (2 ft). Purple globe-shaped flowers in summer.
An extremely useful culinary herb that is reasonably fast growing and grows well in most conditions.

COMFREY (*Symphytum officinale*)
Hardy evergreen perennial; s/p.sh. Height up to 1 m (3 ft). Mauve flowers in spring.
A potentially invasive plant, the claims made about its medicinal properties are endless. Comfrey produces a long tap root, making it unsuitable for containers. The soil needs to be well drained, neutral and very fertile.

FENNEL (*Foeniculum vulgare*)
Hardy perennial; s. Height around 1.5 m (5–6 ft). Yellow flowers in late summer.
A large fast-growing plant, ideal for adding structure and texture to a bed or large container. Prefers drier conditions.

FEVERFEW (*Tanacetum parthenium*)
Hardy perennial; s/p.sh. Height up to 60 cm (2 ft). White flowers in summer.
Famous for its medicinal usage in curing migraines, this plant is a vigorous grower in most well-drained soils. With its golden-green leaves, *T.p.* 'Aureum' is particularly attractive.

ENGLISH LAVENDER (*Lavendula angustifolia*)
Hardy evergreen shrub; s. Height up to 1 m (3 ft). Pink/mauve flowers in midsummer.
A fast-growing evergreen which adds colour and scent to a garden. Prefers non-acidic, drier soils.

LEMON BALM (*Melissa officinalis*)
Hardy perennial; s. Height up to 1 m (3 ft). Yellow/white flowers throughout the summer.
A strongly scented plant often used for making herbal teas in the past. Grows well in most soils but prefers a damp environment.

MARJORAM (*Origanum majorana*)
Hardy or half hardy perennial; s/p.sh. Height up to 38 cm (15 ins). White/purple flowers in late summer.
This herb prefers a dry non-acidic soil and was especially popular in the Middle Ages. Some varieties, such as *O. laevigatum*, do not possess strongly aromatic leaves and are not grown for culinary use. Insects and bees find this plant attractive.

has been caused by too much alcohol! Perhaps it was for this reason that this was one of the nine herbs held sacred by the Anglo-Saxons. It appears in lists from monasteries over 1,200 years ago.

A plant considered in the monasteries to be a cure-all was angelica (*Angelica archangelica*). As its name indicates, it was considered a gift of Heaven. Every part of the plant can be used, from its distinctive leaves, with their strangely lopsided shape, to the stem and roots. The leaves make a good tea for curing flatulence, while the stems, dried and then coated with sugar, make a wonderful decoration on cakes or breads for those special occasions.

CREATING A SENSORY HERB GARDEN

If you prefer a sensory herb garden, then you might consider using some of the more unusual plants with interesting leaves such as lemon balm (*Melissa officinalis*), with its dappled leaves, good for teas or salads, feverfew (*Tanacetum*

MINT (*Mentha* spp.)
Hardy perennial; s/p.sh/sh. Height up to 1 m (3 ft).
A vigorous-growing herb with many varieties which can be invasive. The plant has many culinary and medicinal uses.

NASTURTIUM (*Tropaeolum majus*)
Hardy annual; s/p.sh.
Red/yellow/orange flowers from late summer into autumn.
This highly colourful plant makes an excellent addition to a herb garden. The flowers and leaves can be eaten in salads.

PARSLEY (*Petroselinum crispum*)
Hardy biennial; s/p.sh. Height up to 1 m (3 ft).
This culinary plant needs fertile moist soil to thrive and then can grow quickly. The leaves are particularly attractive and add height and shape to a garden. The plant is usually grown as an annual.

ROSEMARY (*Rosmarinus officinalis*)
Hardy evergreen shrub; s/p.sh. Height up to 1.5 m (5 ft). Blue flowers in spring.
An aromatic shrub which is very amenable: can be grown into hedges and is equally at home in containers. Needs careful pruning to prevent the plants becoming leggy. Many medicinal and culinary uses.

SAGE (*Salvia officinalis*)
Hardy evergreen shrub; s/p.sh. Height up to 60 cm (2 ft).
A herb, probably introduced by the Romans, which will grow in most well-drained soils. Some varieties produce mauve flowers in midsummer but the plant is worth including in a garden simply for its colour and structure.

COMMON THYME (*Thymus vulgaris*)
Hardy evergreen shrub; s. Height up to 30 cm (12 ins). Red/white/purple flowers in summer.
A popular plant well known for its medicinal and culinary uses, thyme

will grow well in most soils that are well drained and provides excellent ground cover or can be a trailing plant in containers.

WINTER SAVORY (*Satureja montana*)
Hardy evergreen shrub; s. Height up to 1 m (3 ft). White flowers in midsummer.
This plant is highly aromatic with many culinary and medicinal uses. It has been used as both an antiseptic and an aphrodisiac. Winter savory needs an alkaline soil and has a tendency to become woody if not pruned back in spring.

YARROW (*Achillea millefolium*)
Hardy perennial; s/p.sh. Height up to 1 m (3 ft). White/pink flowers in summer.
A hardy plant with feathery leaves commonly found growing wild in grass and hedgerows. Used as an aid to digestion and for curing colds.

parthenium), recommended for migraine, bay (*Laurus nobilis*) with its deep green glossy leaves – yellow in late spring – from which oil can be produced to heal bruises or, if added to bathwater, to soothe aches and pains. Tricolour sage, a variegated form of *Salvia officinalis*, has green creamy and deep red striped leaves and is used for a wide range of medical treatments.

These plants will not only be useful for culinary or medicinal purposes but will also provide a soft architectural structure to the planting scheme. Consider adding nasturtiums (*Tropaeolum majus*) with their delightful yellow trumpet and circular leaves. Every part of the plant can be used; they are especially good in salads or as flavourings. Wild strawberries (*Fragaria vesca*) both look beautiful, so delicate and small, and taste marvellous.

I like to have sensory herbs by my front door so that in the evening, when people come home or to visit, the smells fill the air. My culinary herbs are in the back garden, near the kitchen door, for obvious reasons! The great thing about Christian gardens is that they can be symbolic, but they are also highly practical. We are, after all, building upon the symbolic but ultimately practical experiences of the monks and nuns of nearly 1,700 years of Christian monasticism.

However, you can also create a delightful herb garden of the sensory, healing or culinary kind indoors. A herb garden box might sound odd, but so many herbs are suitable for the small scale of an indoor box. The first step is to look at the size of the box and see how many plants you could fit into it. One of the most common mistakes when planting a container, hanging basket or window box is to underplant it. In such a small area the plants must be the central features with the pot or box merely acting as a frame for them.

Once again the sensory aspects of gardens should be taken into consideration and this is really quite simple with herb garden boxes. The more common herbs such as thyme (*Thymus vulgaris*), with its lovely cluster of small flowers and use in tea for 'flu and colds, and mint such as spearmint, *Mentha spicata*, or peppermint, *Mentha piperita,* with their colourful flowerheads and their fine

LEFT: *In the monastic garden areas were often divided into squares to emphasise geometry. This herb garden features squares of thyme, dianthus and rosemary*

scent, are obvious choices when deciding on plants to include in the container.

In practical terms most herbs will grow quite readily in most conditions, although a well-drained soil in sun or partial shade is ideal. Containers need more attention than, say, a planted bed, as they have a tendency to dry out very fast. Regular watering and the occasional feed are essential. You might try mulching around the base of the plants with gravel as this helps to retain the moisture and prevent weed growth.

Once you have planted your window box or container, don't forget to use the herbs. Fresh herbs, newly chopped, are full of flavour and the act of tending your little garden will not only help the box or container retain its structure but will also serve as a method of relaxation. When you leave the window open for a few minutes, the smell of the herbs will quickly permeate the room.

The Symbolism of Monastic Gardens

A feature of monastic gardening was the importance of symbolism. Plants were not seen as just botanical, but as symbols of the Christian life. They came to be given good or bad natures because of either their appearance or effects. Through their resemblance to other things, they also took on a 'sympathetic' dimension, that is to say, if a plant looked like something else it was considered to be linked to it.

An example would be the mandrake, *Mandragora officinarum*, which is shaped like a human, with phallic-shaped roots. Mandrake was used for aphrodisiac purposes – the Bible tells us that Jacob's wives fought over the use of mandrakes to get his attention! Mandrake was also thought to be a miniature of the human form and thus 'good' as a defence against evil, which could be fooled into going into the mandrake root rather than into the person. Another example is lungwort (*Pulmonaria officinalis*). It was used to treat diseases of the lung because its leaves were thought to resemble lungs. The colour of flowers was also considered important. Red flowers were used to treat bleeding while yellow flowers were used to treat jaundice.

Monastic gardens were also, in a sense, theme gardens, due to the symbolic and astrological/spiritual attributes of the flowers, plants and trees.

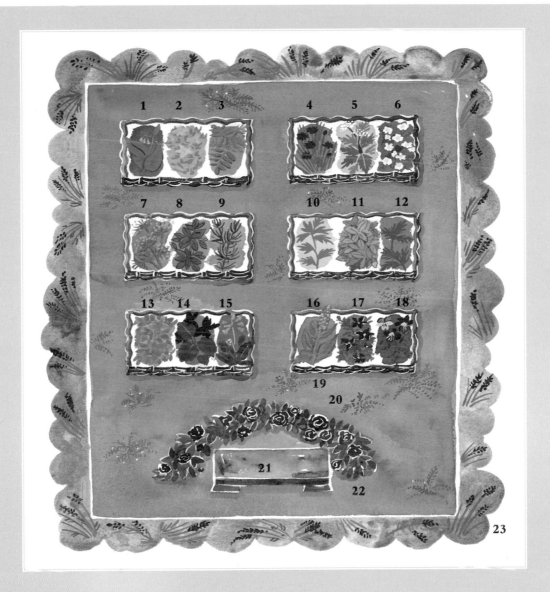

Key

HEALING SECTION
1 Comfrey (*Symphytum officinale*)
2 St John's wort (*Hypericum perforatum*)
3 Liquorice (*Glycyrrhiza glabra*)
4 Chives (*Allium schoenoprasum*)
5 Valerian (*Valeriana officinalis*)
6 Feverfew (*Tanacetum parthenium*))

CULINARY SECTION
7 Fennel (*Foeniculum vulgare*)
8 Peppermint (*Mentha piperita*)
9 Rosemary (*Rosmarinus officinalis*)
10 Lovage (*Levisticum officinalis*)
11 Lemon balm (*Melissa officinalis*)
12 Parsley (*Petroselinum crispum*)

BEAUTY/SENSORY SECTION
13 Sweet marjoram (*Origanum marjorana*)

14 Sweet violet (*Viola odorata*)
15 Mullein (*Verbascum thapsus*)
16 Cowslip (*Primula veris*)
17 Periwinkle (*Vinca minor*)
18 Wild pansy (*Viola tricolor*)

19 Woven wattle fence
20 Camomile path
21 Seat
22 Rose arbour
23 Lavender hedge

CELTIC GARDENS: THE SPIRIT WITHIN NATURE

In Britain, monastic gardens and horticulture were fed by the rich stream of Benedictine monasticism and by the stronger and perhaps even more powerful strand of Celtic Christianity.

Putting it very simply, the Benedictines looked at the collapsed ecosystem of the post-Roman era and decided it needed taking in hand in God's Name. The Celtic Christians, usually living beyond the areas dominated by the old Roman Empire, saw nature as wild and wonderful and speaking of God. They felt that they had a place within this, but it was a humble place. In England, Celtic Christianity flourished from the 4th century AD until the mid 7th to early 8th century in England. In Scotland it lasted until the 10th or 11th century and in Wales even later.

They had gardens, for example the extraordinary ones on Skellig Michael, off the coast of Kerry in Ireland. This tiny island consists of two massive peaks (186 m [610 ft] and 217 m [713 ft] high), at the base of which a monastery was founded in the 7th century. On this barren, windswept spot the monks clung to the rock face and yet still managed to create tiny gardens, carrying soil from the mainland 19 km (12 miles) away.

The Celtic vision of nature was a mystical one, linking back to the pre-Christian Druidic sense of being within nature, and their gardens expressed this. The images found in prayers, poems and hymns depict places of solitude, hedged around to keep out winds, noise and wild animals. Trees, flowers, and of course herbs and vegetables, were the staples of these gardens. But they do not appear to have been the regular, rather grandiose and planned monastery gardens of the Roman Church. These were small scale, homely places, where the monk or hermit provided space, food, water and shelter

SYMBOLISM AND THE MEDIEVAL GARDEN

LEFT: Colourful borders can bring an echo of monasticism into a modern garden. Favourite medieval flowers to plant could include dianthus, lavender and lily of the valley.

Every aspect of the medieval garden was imbued with rich symbolism, from the flowers and plants, to the lawns and fountains. The fountain was seen as symbolic of the Holy Trinity for water was found in three different forms: water bubbled at the head of the fountain, it fell in droplets to the pool, and rippled gently in the pool. The lawn was seen as deeply symbolic, representing in its green colour rebirth and eternal life. The turf itself would often be divided into four squares

representing the four corners of the Earth. However, perhaps it is the flowers, often allowed to bloom freely in a garden's mead, that hold the most potent symbolism. Violets were symbolic of humility, daisies represented innocence and irises symbolised faith, wisdom and courage in their three pairs of petals. The rose, however, was held in highest regard. The Virgin Mary's purity was symbolised by the white rose, while the blood of Christ was represented by the red rose.

for all manner of God's creatures, from the birds to the beasts. They were slightly wild – like Eden gone a little to seed!

THE MEDIEVAL PLEASURE GARDEN

By medieval times, the relationship with the Divine was fixed and hierarchical. The nobility were able to celebrate their exalted position in pleasure gardens.

From what we can glean from paintings and scant remains on the ground, these gardens were a series of enclosed or semi-enclosed areas within a walled setting. Trellises, topiaried hedges, trees, high walls, turf seats and colonnades divided the garden into distinct, if not to say discreet, areas. Here ladies could wander and men loiter. The pleasure garden features greatly in the romantic poems and literature of the Middle Ages – part Paradise, part Eden, part symbol of woman's sexuality, part symbol of natural innocence. The overlay of images is immense and highly sensual. Perhaps we can say with some accuracy that by the 15th century, gardens in England and northern Europe had become not only sacred but also secret and sensual!

Today, the revival of monastic, Christ-centred gardens is a feature of sacred gardening

Eventually, the pleasure gardens, secret gardens and great parks of the nobles overcame the spiritual, pragmatic and mystic gardens of the monasteries. The Reformation destroyed these centres of good practice and the landed gentry took control. It might seem that sacred gardens were on their way out. As explicit places attached to explicitly sacred buildings, to a great extent this was true. But the sacred has always found a way of expressing itself.

Today, the return or revival of monastic, Christ-centred gardens is a noticeable feature of sacred gardening. The Reformation, revolutions and urban spread may have destroyed the great monastic gardens of the past. But their spirit, their insights, their vision of humanity, God and all creation in harmony are qualities which we are finding we need to reinstate. This is a recovered wisdom, which we are learning to understand anew as we seek to repair the damage done to our world – and to ourselves – by attitudes of arrogance and presumption in the way we have related to nature. Their recovery and re-creation forms truly sacred gardening. In the next chapter you will find some inspiring examples of how to incorporate these ideas into your own garden.

MEDIEVAL PLANTING

The following plants have been documented as having been used either medicinally or aesthetically in noble medieval gardens. They are just as popular today.

COLUMBINE (*Aquilegia vulgaris*)
This delicate plant, bearing purple, white, pink or blue flowers in early summer, grows best in partial shade. It will grow to nearly a metre (2–3 ft) in height and will thrive in most soils, apart from highly acidic ones. The beautiful flowers do not last long. Dead-head immediately after flowering.

COWSLIP (*Primula veris*)
This popular native plant, once common in semi-natural grassland, is making a comeback in the wild. The clusters of yellow flowers are a beautiful sight in the spring. The origin of its common name varies from the rather fanciful idea that it is derived from the flower's scent – supposedly like a cow's breath – to the slightly more likely but less attractive proposition that it is a euphemism for cow-pat.

LAVENDER (*Lavendula* spp.)
Lavender is one of the most familiar of garden plants and rightly so. Apart from its mauve flowers in midsummer, used in oils and pot pourri, this plant provides wonderful grey-blue foliage that is intensely aromatic. In medieval times it would have been grown in a herber or along the edges of gardens so that the scent would be released when someone brushed past. It will grow in most soils but prefers a limy, sandy soil.

LILY OF THE VALLEY (*Convallaria majalis*)
The bell-shaped white flowers of this plant which appear in late spring are one of the most welcome sights of the gardening year. Lily of the valley grows naturally in many deciduous woodlands and on a still sunny day fills the air with its wonderful aroma. It will grow in most soils providing that there is partial shade and good drainage.

MALE FERN (*Dryopteris filix-mas*)
Possibly the best architectural plants for a garden are the ferns and this is a great example. It is probably the most common of all British native ferns and grows well in damp shady places. The fronds are up to a metre (3 ft) in length and are vivid green in colour.

PEONY (*Paeonia officinalis*)
This beautiful perennial is also known as 'Roman Peony' and has deep red exotic flowers in early summer. It will thrive in any well-drained fertile soil and even after its flowering period the beautiful finger-like leaves add height and form to a border. The plant grows up to around 60 cm (2 ft) in height.

ROSE (*Rosa gallica* var. *officinalis; Rosa × Alba*)
The *Rosa gallica* var. *officinalis* is also known as 'the apothecary's rose' and 'the red rose of Lancaster'. It is without doubt one of the oldest of a very ancient family of roses and was often linked with the Madonna, more often than not in contrast to the lily. It has scarlet flowers in early summer and grows up to a metre (3 ft) in height.
Rosa × alba is another very old rose, also known as 'the white rose of York'. As the name suggests, it has white flowers in the summer. There are a number of other types of Alba, such as *Rosa × 'Alba Maxima'* ('Jacobite Rose'), *Rosa × Alba 'Alba Semiplena'* and 'Great Maiden's Blush', all of which would have been available to the medieval gardener.

SWEET ROCKET (*Hesperis matronalis*)
Sweet rocket is a tall (1 m [3 ft]) biennial which is a native of Italy. It was grown in noble gardens mainly for its sweet-smelling pink or white flowers, which are borne throughout midsummer. The plant will grow anywhere in full sun or partial shade and benefits from planting in drifts.

SWEET VIOLET (*Viola odorata*)
This attractive ground-hugging plant is best grown in partial shade and either at the front of beds or as general ground cover. The purple or white flowers are strongly scented, hence the name, and appear early in the year. The plant will tolerate most soils provided they are moist.

VINE (*Vitis vinifera*)
Not only were these climbers grown for their grapes but they also became one of the most popular climbing plants for arbours. In Britain the grapes are often not of the quality of those grown in warmer climates, but if situated in a sunny spot a vine will grow without the help of a greenhouse. This plant is ideal for growing on an arbour, pergola or trellis; like most climbers, it needs support. Grapes should appear in late summer, with most of the leaf growth coming a little earlier. Careful attention should be paid to pruning. The purple-leaved vine, *V. vinifera* 'Purpurea', makes an attractive alternative and may also produce grapes.

3

CHRISTIAN GARDENS TODAY

The Christian garden was a feature of our landscape for centuries, focused upon the monastic life. Today, through churchyards managed for wildlife, themed gardens and meditational Christian gardens, or through being able to 'read' the symbolism of plants and trees, the Christian garden is reappearing.

The tradition of Christian gardens is found in the Easter garden (see page 66), or the association of certain trees with the Passion of Christ (see page 67). The Passion has the Garden of Gethsemane as its focus and the garden motif is continued to the garden tomb where, according to Scripture, Jesus was buried.

Christianity is incomprehensible without its Jewish roots, and in discussing 'Christian' gardens we need to acknowledge that much of the inspiration for them comes from Judaism and from the Hebrew Bible. It is of course from Judaism that the notion of a special garden comes, from the story of the Garden of Eden (see Chapter 1). Judaism also provides the idea of the centrality of the tree – the Tree of the Knowledge of Good and Evil in the Garden of Eden, which in Christian thought is replaced by the tree of Calvary, the wooden cross on which Christ was crucified.

FEATURES OF CHRISTIAN GARDENS

Today in Israel and in other centres of Jewish life, such as the United States of America, Jewish Biblical gardens can be found which contain plants mentioned in the Hebrew Bible. For example, there are a number of shrubs which tradition has defined as the Burning Bush from which God spoke. These include the summer cypress (*Bassia scoparia*), which turns a vibrant red or yellow in the summer, depending on the amount of rainfall, and the oil-exuding *Dictamnus albus*. However, because for many centuries Jews were forbidden to establish great religious land-holding centres comparable to the great monasteries with their land holdings, or even to have the sort of life style which enabled the growth of gardens, the creation of sacred gardens in Judaism is relatively new. In this chapter we shall draw inspiration from the Jewish roots of Christian gardens, but focus upon the wider range of sacred garden traditions within Christianity.

Christian gardens can be seen as falling into three main categories. First, there are the symbolic gardens, which were most clearly seen in the monastic layout (see Chapter 2). Secondly, Christian gardens are thematic. They tell a story.

For centuries, Easter gardens have done this, as we shall see on page 67. Today gardens are increasingly being designed as an aid to meditation and reflection, appealing to the visitor through a series of ideas and narratives such as the life of Christ or the story of Mary. Such reflective gardens have long been a feature of retreat centres and monasteries or of shrines. You will find them at Catholic retreat centres, for example, where they may be a stations of the cross walk, where the 14 stations or incidents on Christ's walk from the trial to his Crucifixion are depicted in sculpture along a walk through woods and flowers.

Thirdly, Christian gardens are pragmatic. In a monastery some of the ingredients for hospitality or healing were grown in the herb garden; in churchyards the dead lie buried or commemorated in what is often referred to as 'God's acre'. These often ancient sites are indeed sacred spaces, enclosed when the land was meadowland and untouched since by farming or pesticides. They are eco-systems which, through careful handling, can be made sanctuaries for wildlife ranging from birds, butterflies and insects to hedgehogs, slow-worms and bats.

The popularity of gardens of Biblical plants or the creation of Biblically themed gardens such as the one outside Jerusalem, (see page 64) all bear witness to a centuries-old and continuing relationship between Christianity and the garden.

THE FEAST OF LIFE

The Christian faith is one which takes the creation seriously. The belief that God became human to live amongst us means that Christianity looks upon the physical, created world as a realm of God's glory and as dear to God's heart. For this reason, a basic theme in Christian gardening is celebration – celebration of the wonders of creation, of our place within it and of God's love for it. It is this sense of sharing in celebration and in creation which informs the Living Churchyards Project, turning graveyards into places where nature can co-exist with humanity. It has inspired the creation festivals which so many churches and cathedrals have celebrated, rejoicing in the beauties of nature but in so doing becoming more acutely aware of the ills that affect the natural world today.

The popularity of church flower festivals picks up on this theme, using the natural materials of the church, often made from local stone, as a backdrop to a visual feast of nature. These flower festivals often choose a Christian theme such as the Resurrection, or the life of St. Francis as a basis for the designs.

A Feast of Life garden reminds us to celebrate the healing, life-giving, taste-giving, pleasure-giving powers that God has given to the plants, flowers and trees. You may want to turn part of your own garden into such a special, celebratory place.

In planning a Feast of Life garden, bear one important insight in mind: Christianity teaches that we are co-creators with God. In our hands lies the power to create beauty or destroy beauty. In our hands we have the strength to plant or dig up. We can plan a garden which is not just of joy to us, but also to creation generally. Our Feast of Life garden should echo the old Muslim teaching, first stated by the Prophet Mohammed, that who so ever plants a tree performs an act of charity, for it will provide homes for birds and insects, food for other creatures and shade for us.

A basic theme in Christian gardening is celebration of the wonders of creation.

Look at your Feast of Life garden as a feast you are preparing for the birds, insects, mammals, butterflies, bats and other wildlife of your area. See it as home and sanctuary to endangered plant species. This does not mean dig them up and transplant them! But one important aspect of Christian gardens is to nurture rarer species from seed and to provide a place where the plants which modern farming has pushed to the edge can find rest and sanctuary. This will obviously depend upon what type of soil

you have. But try to plan your garden to take account of endangered plant species or species which have lost much of their traditional land through building or intensive agriculture. You might also create a pond or stream which can support a frog and toad colony. The disappearance of these amphibians is a sad sign of the unhealthiness of our environment. They also act as excellent pest controls!

Provide plenty of tree or shrub cover for birds to feed from, especially those trees and shrubs which will provide berries for birds through the autumn or winter. *Skimmia japonica* has bright red berries which are produced throughout winter, as has the spotted laurel (*Aucuba japonica*). You may also need to place nesting boxes on inaccessible walls or high in mature trees to ensure a safe breeding-place for birds.

It is also worth having a 'wild area', an area where you mow the grass less regularly, allow brambles to trail and wander, old wood to rot. Such areas of wilderness provide a haven for many creatures, especially in rotting wood. But equally importantly they are a reminder of our humility before God. It was customary in the great cathedrals and synagogues, to leave one part of the building either unfinished, or in a rough and ready state. This reminds us that only God can build the perfect creation – a reminder that one or two gardeners I know might like to heed!

The essential nature of a Feast of Life garden is to have diversity, sanctuary, wilderness, water and beauty. To plan this is obviously primarily a personal thing. But a rather good method is to have the six days of creation as your motif. To do this, you will need to look at the space you have available and allocate it appropriately. You may choose to sit in one place and see all 'six days' at once, rather like God in Heaven, or stroll from one to the next, as Genesis tells us God did!

The six days are as follows:

Day One

The first day saw the creation of light over water. The first three days require the presence of water, as does the fifth. Therefore make a stream or, even better, a pond or small lake the centrepiece of your garden. This is also an important reminder that we are 90% water ourselves and that the majority

LEFT: This profusion of white roses evokes the blessings of creation in a Feast of Life garden, while the tumbling wall can be the basis for a Jericho garden (see page 61).

of the planet is covered with water. Without water there is no life. So, if you can, plan a pond which begins with a large space at the end.

Here we need the bright light that begins creation. I like the idea of a forsythia such as *Forsythia × intermedia* with its bright yellow flowers. The burst of colour that a good forsythia gives is like the burst of light at the start of creation. The fact that the forsythia breaks into flower so early in the year in the northern hemisphere makes it a symbol of the start of life each spring, which in turn mirrors the start of life on Day One. Plant your forsythia to overhang the water and to be reflected back to you.

Day Two

On the second day God created the Heavens over the waters. Tall order! But you can do this with an arched trellis over the next section of the pond. Climbing roses, especially if they are of the Old English kind and of small size, give a wonderful sense of beauty and light firmness. Bear in mind that foliage around ponds can be troublesome – the leaf litter will need to be cleaned out in the spring. If you have limited time available you may find an evergreen which can lean out over the waters an attractive answer!

Day Three

Day Three saw the creation of dry land and the coming of the grasses, plants with seeds and fruit trees. The scope here is limitless and this is where you can begin to incorporate the planting of rarer species. As for the dry land, I like the idea of the pond breaking around a long spit of land which eventually leads us out of the pond on Day Six to *terra firma*. If you have the space, what a wonderful thing to design! Luxuriance is what we are looking for here – willow trees such as the weeping willow (*Salix babylonica*) spilling into the water; water lilies (*Nymphaea* spp. or *Nymphaeoides peltatum*) clustering around the first touch of the spit of land; tall grasses and a scattering of flowers such as pansies (the *Viola* family), periwinkles (*Vinca major*) or bluebells (*Hyacinthoides non-scripta*). As for fruit trees, this depends on the size of your garden and the type of soil. For average-sized gardens an apple tree is a good choice and brings with it powerful Christian associations.

Day Four

On the fourth day God created the sun and moon, so the theme here is white and yellow flowers. The choice is immense – for the sun, anything from meadow buttercups (*Ranunculus acris*) and St.

The burst of colour provided by a forsythia can represent the burst of light at Creation.

John's wort (*Hypericum perforatum*) to rose of Sharon (*Hypericum calycinum*) and yellow-horned poppies (*Glaucium flavum*). For the moon, the choice ranges from pignut (*Conopodium majus*) with its delicate umbrella of colour and edible roots, through wood-sorrel (*Oxalis acetosella*), whose delicate shape and flowering during Easter have long associated it with the Resurrection, to white roses.

This could be the area for your rotting wood and overgrown wildness, amongst, on top of and through which the sun and moon colours emerge as splashes of colour.

Day Five

This was when the creatures of the water were created. Make your pond a place of aquatic life for fish, frogs, toads, even newts if you can, a sanctuary for some of these threatened or diminishing species.

Day Six

This saw the creation of the creatures of the land – land which offers a home for all manner of creatures, including of course humanity. To mark this allow space for a garden seat under a bower of trees, resting on a grass lawn or overlooking beds of flowers a little way from the water.

You are the creator, with God, in this Feast of Life. Celebrate the wonders of life in your Feast of Life garden and join God in 'wandering in the garden in the cool of the evening'.

THE JERICHO GARDEN

Biblically themed gardens can come in many different forms. They may, for example, take a point in the history of Israel and dwell upon that. I have seen a very effective 'Jericho garden'. This is a garden based around an old, tumbled down wall, but you could equally well use old bricks or even tiles, so long as you make what is in effect a rockery which seems to have tumbled down. If you have the materials sufficient to produce the sense of a wall that has a gap in it, this strengthens the sense of the walls of Jericho, through whose breaches the trumpeting Israelites streamed to capture the city and thus enter the Promised Land.

The image of the walls of Jericho tumbling down has long been used in Christian reflection as an interior motif. We build walls – between ourselves and others, ourselves and God, ourselves and the world – indeed, even between parts of our own nature and personality. The collapse of the walls to the clarion call instituted by God speaks to us of the need for some walls to fall before new life can re-emerge; the importance of clearing away old habits or ways of thinking. Your Jericho garden can speak to you of this truth.

Tumbledown old walls overgrown with plants are always attractive. Creepers such as the *Hedera canariensis* ivy, with its white, creamy variegated leaves, form a lovely basic ground growth, strengthening the sense of an upright wall fallen down. For a similar but slightly more unusual effect you might try growing a clematis horizontally, rather than as a climber, or the *Clematis montana* for a fast result over a long wall.

Another splendid Jericho garden made a feature of 'trumpet' flowers such as daffodils. *Narcissus*, especially *Narcissus cyclamineus,* or jonquil offer a delightful show if planted in the better soil around the edges of the wall. The colourful tobacco plant (*Nicotiana affinis*), which gives off such a delightful scent in the evening air, is another trumpet flower. To emphasise the wall motif, plant wallflowers (*Erysimum cheiri*) with their different colours of red, orange, yellow, copper and purple. They come in different sizes to suit the scale and size of your site.

A DESERT OR WILDERNESS GARDEN

A desert garden can also reflect a Biblical theme and a monastic insight. By 'desert' I don't just mean a garden created in a desert, but one created in hostile conditions such as a stony beach or in the damaged soil of brown-field sites (previously built upon land which has lost its fertility). The most common type of desert garden is one which acknowledges the exhausted, damaged or even polluted nature of the land. It thus becomes a place to practise what the Celtic monks called 'Green martyrdom'.

From the 5th century onwards the Celtic monastic tradition was deeply influenced by the monasticism and asceticism of Egyptian monks. Contacts between the two traditions, completely bypassing Rome, are well recorded. Christian monasticism began in Egypt when in the mid 4th century great ascetic saints such as St. Anthony, retreated from the urban, urbane, cosmopolitan and corrupt great cities such as Alexandria, into the desert. Here the monks sought God in solitude and struggle with the self. When the Egyptian monastic tradition came to the Celtic lands of Ireland, Wales and Cornwall, the Celtic monks sought their own deserts – areas of wilderness, barrenness and isolation. Indeed, to this day you will find out of the way places in Ireland or Wales called Dissert or Dessert as reminders of this quest.

If you find yourself grappling with damaged land in your own garden, you can turn this desert tradition to new use. Here in your small patch of polluted soil or rubble-strewn land, you have the chance to create a Kingdom

THE LABYRINTH AS CHRISTIAN METAPHOR

The labyrinth is one of the most potent of Christian symbols, although the origins of the labyrinth date well before Christianity. A labyrinth has been found carved into rock in the island of Sardinia which is over 4,000 years old, and most of us familiar with the labyrinth described in the Greek myth of Theseus and the Minotaur. According to legend the labyrinth held the Minotaur, half man, half bull at its centre. The Christian Church introduced an 11–ring labyrinth which represented the 11 true apostles. The labyrinth symbolised the journey of the soul from darkness into light, and during the Crusades was seen as representing the dangers and uncertainties of the pilgrim's path to Jerusalem. One of the most famous Christian labyrinths is set in the floor of Chartres Cathedral: its path takes 200 metres to trace. To create your own adaptation of a labyrinth see page 129.

LEFT: *The Cretan Seven Circuit, the labyrinth described in the Greek myth of Theseus and the Minotaur.*

RIGHT: *The Celtic Triple Spiral*

of God – a place of recovery and of struggle, a place where every plant's foothold is a minor miracle of survival and tender love. Although he had no such overt Christian purpose, the beach garden of the film-maker and actor Derek Jarman is an example of a marvellous wilderness garden, now lovingly maintained by his former partner following his death. Take pride in your own minor miracles of reclamation and regeneration. Instead of feeling a failure when most of your plants do not thrive, feel a sense of achievement in the few that do. In this is a metaphor of the Christian life as spelt out by Jesus in his parable of the sower. Read Matthew, Chapter 13:3–23.

Most of our wildflowers will grow in poor soil conditions. In fact, for many species, the poorer the soil, the better. The ox-eye daisy (*Leucanthemum vulgare*), poppy (*Papaver rhoeas*), broom (*Cytisus* spp.), or sea holly (*Eryngium maritimum*) will make a terrific show in your desert garden.

In a Dallas church garden I recall the simple use of rock, sand and cacti, with a mechanically produced stream flowing to bring to mind John the Baptist, who baptised in the river Jordan, lived in the hills and was someone Herod found to be somewhat prickly! A Christian garden can be fun and filled with puns and jokes as well as be a place of serious reflection. The Christian life is after all a celebration that even in the most adverse conditions, love, hope and, I would argue, fun can emerge.

If your garden area boasts a large rock, this could be your Mount Sinai. Around it you could grow smaller flowers such as saxifrages and gentians, which are best suited to thin soil.

THE LIFE OF CHRIST GARDEN

Just to the north of the old city of Jerusalem lies a strange shrine. Here, close to a major road near the bus station, is the Garden Tomb, a tomb which that highly eccentric yet strangely attractive 19th-century character, General Gordon, believed was really the tomb of Jesus. Like many Protestants, he found the overcrowded and squabbled over Church of the Holy Sepulchre unbearable. It was not the sort of sacred space he wanted. Instead he went looking for a more 'genuine' experience, an encounter with the Christ he felt he knew. He also went looking for 'a hill outside the city wall', perhaps not worrying too much that the city wall had moved many times since the time of Jesus!

He found what he was looking for in a deserted quarry. Here he discovered what is indeed a circa 1st-century tomb, cut into the rock face. Inside are the remains of resting-places and stone ledges for the dead. And here it was that Gordon declared Jesus had been buried and risen again.

Few people today argue that this site is genuine. But who can dismiss the peace, beauty and the sense of simplicity it provides? For many, this tomb offers a much stronger sense of the death and Resurrection of Christ than does the chaotic diversity of the Church of the Holy Sepulchre.

The tomb itself is interesting, of course, but it is the environment that has been created around it which is the more interesting still. For here is a perfect 'English' garden. It is laid out with plants, some Biblical but not all, and quotes from the Scriptures, with places for worship and places for quiet contemplation. Through very skilful landscaping and planting, a small area has been turned into a garden of hidden depths and corners, where, on my last visit, six different groups of about 20 people in each group, from the Philippines, Sweden, England, the USA, Jamaica and Hong Kong, were able to worship, sing, even dance, in separate spaces and still leave quiet areas for a lone visitor such as myself. Through the layout of the landscape and the choice of trees and plants, this relatively small area creates a sense of peace and has become a garden of the Passion of Christ.

Not everyone can find a 1st-century rock tomb around which to create a garden focusing on the life of Christ. But through the use of symbolism, even a small urban garden can become a journey into the life and signifi-

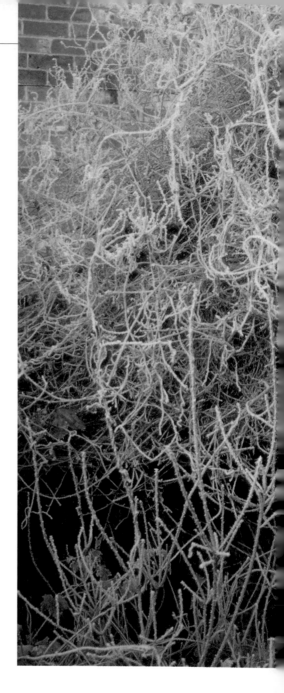

ABOVE: This simple statue of Mary stands in a grotto overgrown with a frost-covered vine. Discreet seating provides a perfect area for reflection.

cance of Jesus Christ. I have already mentioned a garden where a thorn tree
dominated the East. This dense tree drew your eye and brought to mind
both the crown of thorns and the tree of the Crucifixion. But beneath it was
planted an array of bulbs which emerged from the ground at Easter to celebrate the Resurrection. The tree itself was covered with blossom at much
the same time.

In my own garden, I have planted a tree each Good Friday. The main
tree, which dominates the eastern side of my garden is, very appropriately,
a Christmas-flowering cherry. In the depth of winter it brings intense joy

with its delicate flowers. I plant on Good Friday because putting into the ground that which will soar above it and turning the tree of death of the Crucifixion into a living symbol of life is a wonderful way of observing Christianity's most awe-ful day. Christ himself spoke about the power of the imagery of the seed buried in the ground which grows into the tree. In Matthew 13:31–32 he says:

> 'The Kingdom of Heaven is like a mustard seed which a man took and sowed in his field. It is the smallest of seeds, but when it has grown it is the biggest shrub of all and becomes a tree so that the birds of the air come and shelter in its branches.'

So, even in a small garden, by using a tree or shrub, you can provide a focus which draws your eye and perhaps your heart to the East, the direction of Jerusalem, of Golgotha and of another tree, 2,000 years ago.

If you have the space, then a combination of trees or bushes can capture the beginning and then the climax of the life of Christ. In the northern hemisphere, a Christmas-flowering bush or tree, such as the winter sweet (*Chimonanthus praecox*), with its sweet-smelling creamy and purple flowers, celebrates the birth of hope in the midst of winter. You might also try a witch hazel (*Hamamelis mollis*) which puts out exotic rich yellow flowers around Christmas time. In the southern hemisphere the Australian Christmas bush (*Ceratopetallum gummiferum*) has white flowes followed by red seeds at around Christmas, while the Pohutukawa (*Metrosideros excelsa*) is the New Zealand Christmas Tree.

Beside this plant a Glastonbury May hawthorn (*Crataegus monogyna 'Biflora'*), which with its thorns and red berries has long been a symbol of the Passion of Christ. In the northern hemisphere it is May-flowering (hence its other name, the May tree). After Easter when its bare branches show their thorns clearly, it is a symbol of the pain of the Crucifixion, but also of the wonder and glory of the Resurrection.

These two types of trees or shrubs can be a reflective basis for other features which explore Christ's life. For example, the lily of the valley (*Convallaria majalis*) recalls the teaching of Christ that not even Solomon in all his glory is as beautifully dressed as this gift of God. Herbs for healing remind one of the healings of Christ and of the herbs used to prepare his body for the tomb.

If you have the space at one end of your garden, plant a Christmas-flowering tree or shrub and make a path which leads, via lilies of the valley, herbs and other flowers, to the hawthorn tree. This short walk can encapsulate the life of Christ. Ideally you should incorporate three other features. The first, near the beginning of the path, is water to represent the river Jordan in which Christ was baptised and also the Sea of Galilee so central to his early life. The second feature is a rock, reminding the visitor of the Mount of Transfiguration where Moses and Elijah appeared side by side with Jesus. Finally comes an Easter garden (see below).

If all this sounds rather daunting, you might find that by accident you have a tree growing in your garden which for centuries has been associated with Jesus. This is the oft-despised elder, *Sambucus nigra*. For over 700 years this has also had the nickname 'the Judas Iscariot', for it was believed that it was from this species of tree that he hanged himself after betraying Christ. But, as if to compensate the tree for such a slur, it was also declared to be the tree from which the wood of the cross was made. So next time an elder pops up and you have to wrestle with its intrusion, reflect a moment that God might be saying something to you!

THE EASTER GARDEN

The idea of a Life of Christ garden is not new. Indeed, one could argue that the Easter garden, celebrating the death and Resurrection of Christ, is one of the longest surviving sacred gardens in the West. Throughout the Middle Ages (if not earlier) and right up to the present, churches across Europe have laid out a special, short lived garden either on Maundy Thursday or Good Friday morning which lasts until the end of Easter week. In some Continental European traditions it remains until Whit Sunday, 50 days after Easter. In some old churches, special Holy Sepulchre tombs were built inside the sanctuary, to the left of the altar (as you face it). Here each Good Friday a small garden was made and/or clothes laid out to symbolise the death and then the Resurrection of Jesus. Outside in the churchyard, Easter gardens are made as a public sign of the faith.

The Easter garden is one of the longest-surviving sacred gardens in the West.

Many Christian families will make their own Easter garden, either in their garden or indoors. In our family, we have always made one at home on Good Friday and we help to create the one at our church on Maundy Thursday. Our Easter garden at home lasts until about a week after Easter.

The idea is to create a miniature version of the garden and tomb. Size is entirely a personal choice, determined as much by space and time as by anything else. The one we build at home is formed around the gently rotting base of an old tree, around a metre (some 3 ft) across. The largest I have ever built was about 250 cm (8 ft) long

and 120 cm (4 ft) deep. It stood to a height of perhaps a metre (3 ft), plus an additional 30 cm (a foot) for the central cross.

Some gardens and churches keep the basic elements of the Easter garden from year to year, allowing moss to grow over the stonework and grass to grown in front of the cave, with other rock or climbing plants to grow as they wish. On Good Friday the crosses and stone blocking the cave are put in place and fresh annual plants (see box) planted ready for Easter Sunday.

The traditional style of an Easter garden requires a base of stone or wood, or a flattish piece of land (note that such constructions in a churchyard need the appropriate authorisation). On this base construct a small rocky hill, the centre of which is the cave of the tomb. Use stones and rocks to create as realistic an appearance as possible. Cover your 'hill' with moss. If you are lucky, this will take root, making it possible to keep the basic structure for year after year. On the summit of the 'hill' place the three crosses of the Crucifixion. These are usually made from twigs or small branches (keep them looking as natural as possible) to represent the tree. The tree represents life and death as well as the tree of the Crucifixion.

We know from John's Gospel that the tomb stood in a garden, for in John 20:11–18, we have the story of how Jesus appeared to Mary Magdalene. At first she did not recognise him, 'supposing him to be the gardener'. Traditionally primroses are used to show the garden, as these flowers have long had an association with Easter. Other 'miniature' flowers and plants such as those listed left can be used. Grasses, moss again or a mixture of pebbles and bark can create a delightful context within which to plant the flowers. I have also seen bonsai trees used well on indoor Easter gardens and they certainly make the scene most 'realistic'. You can add your own personal touch to create a place of real beauty.

THE MARIAN GARDEN

Many monasteries had Marian gardens – flower gardens with flowers associated with the Virgin Mary. The Virgin Mary and gardens were a favourite theme of religious iconography and symbolism of the Middle Ages. This can

SMALL EASTER-FLOWERING PLANTS

The following plants are small flowering plants that are often found in rock and container gardens. Most of these are ground hugging. They all flower in the spring.

ALYSSUM (*Alyssum montanum*)
AUBRIETA (*Aubrieta deltoidea*)
GLORY OF THE SNOW (*Chionodoxa*)
LILY OF THE VALLEY (*Convallaria majalis*)
PRIMULA (*Primula allionii*)
PRIMULA (*Primula* 'Wanda')
ROCK PHLOX (*Phlox douglasii*)
SAXIFRAGE (*Saxifraga apiculata*)
SAXIFRAGE (*Saxifraga moschata*)
SPRING GENTIAN (*Gentiana verna*)

LEFT: Lily of the Valley (Convallaria Majalis) – an eternal symbol of Mary.

still be found in old carols where Mary is compared to plants or flowers, as in 'The Holly and the Ivy'.

Much of what we know of the layout, design and contents of medieval gardens comes from the gardens portrayed in the background of Virgin and Child paintings. This practice led to later medieval artists depicting noble ladies in exactly the same pose in such gardens. The irony is of course that most noble gardens were designed or were supposed to be designed to further the dalliance of romantic love, with hideaways for concealed lovers, secret liaisons and covert exchange of billet-doux.

One has only to look at the number of plants associated with the Virgin Mary or with certain saints such as St. John (especially popular because his feast is midsummer and thus plenty of flowers are out) to see that our ancestors themed their own gardens and plants Biblically! Indeed, it does appear that monastic gardens were sometimes themed in this way, with a special Marian section.

Today, the creation of Marian gardens has become quite popular. They differ greatly, some relying on just statues of the Virgin to give the garden such a theme. But others have been planned to draw out the implicit imagery contained within plants associated with her name.

In particular I like the idea of a rosary garden. The rosary is formed of five decades – 10 beads plus the marker bead. Each bead signifies a 'Hail Mary, Full of Grace' prayer and the eleventh bead is the 'Our Father'. At the end of the five rounds, you say, 'Glory be to God'. The Catholic practice of the rosary is for contemplation and for centring upon Our Lady. But a garden path can do the same. By creating five spaces along a garden path or within your garden and moving from one to the next saying the Hail Mary and Lord's Prayer, you can walk and contemplate the rosary. A medium-sized garden can accommodate this sort of Biblical garden. At each place that you stop, you can plant flowers and plants associated with Mary.

Another approach is to take the theme of the life of Mary and find plants and symbols suitable for each stage. For example, Mary's birth could be featured with white flowers such as lilies or the iceberg rose. Both lilies and roses are traditionally associated with the Virgin. In medieval paintings, she is almost always shown holding or standing near a lily at the Annunciation, when the angel

CREATING A MARIAN GARDEN

This garden features beautiful blue and white flowers, but with other colours used to accent a particular time of year or festival honouring the Virgin. Plan a circular garden paved with golden limestone or golden quartzite chipping to resemble the Virgin's halo and enclosed by an evergreen border of rosemary *Rosmarinus officinalis* 'Mrs Jessop's Upright' or lavender (*Lavendula stoechas* f. *leucantha*). It should feature five sections each separated by its own path as shown in the diagram opposite. All five paths should then connect to a central rose arbour. To help unify the whole design, line the paths with edging plants such as pinks (*Dianthus*) and a mixture of blue and white-flowering periwinkle (*Vinca minor* and *Vinca major* var. alba). The entrance to each section should be planted with an upright conifer such as *Cupressus macrocarpa* 'Gold Crest' or *Juniperus virginiana* 'Burkii'. Each section of the garden represents a decade of the rosary and should commemorate a stage of the Virgin's life: her birth (in the Western calendar celebrated during September), the Annunciation, the purification of Mary after the birth of Jesus (traditionally celebrated at Candlemas in February, the Passion (Easter) and Mary's assumption into Heaven (August). Plant each section with tall flowers at the centre, surrounded by medium-sized flowers and then low-growing ground-covers at the outer edge. The planting scheme opposite is designed for northern hemisphere seasons, however, it can easily be adapted to suit your climate and conditions. For a key to the plants used in each section see page 156.

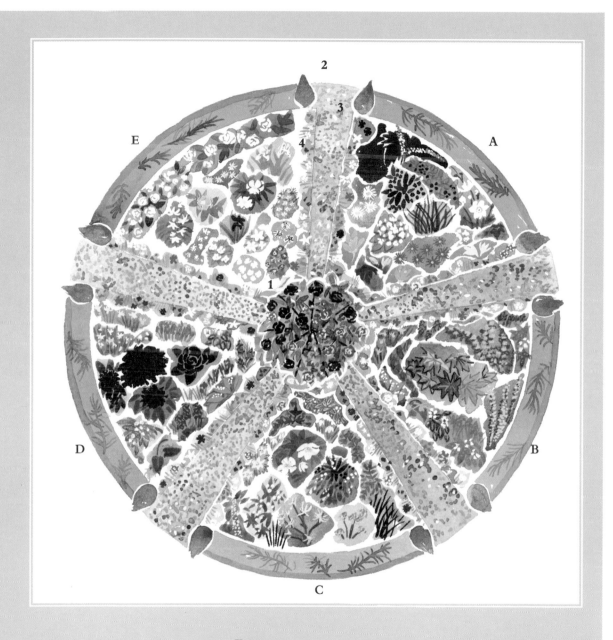

Key

1. Rose arbour
2. Conifer (*Cupressus macrocarpa* 'Gold Crest' or *Juniperus virginiana* 'Burkii')
3. Path
4. Border of pinks (*Dianthus*) and periwinkles (*Vinca* spp)

A Birth section
B Annunciation section
C Purification section
D Passion section
E Assumption section

MARIAN PLANTS

There are literally hundreds of plants that over the centuries have been dedicated to Our Lady and some of the names, such as Lady's mantle (*Alchemilla vulgaris*), survive today. Traditionally Mary has been a symbol of purity and righteousness and many of the plants that are dedicated to her are a reflection of this, such as wild strawberry (*Fragaria vesca*) and the common daisy (*Bellis perennis*). Many common names for plants are prefixed with the word 'Lady's' which in many cases has been shortened from 'Our Lady's', as is the case, for example, with Lady's bedstraw (*Galium verum*).

The following are just a few of the 600 or so plants that are dedicated to Mary:

KEY

s = sun p.sh = partial shade
sh = shade

BIRD'S-FOOT TREFOIL (*Lotus corniculatus*)
Hardy perennial; s/p.sh. Height up to 30 cm (12 ins). Yellow flowers in summer.
Also known as 'Lady's slipper' and 'bacon and eggs', this is a native wild flower often found in grassland. As with harebell, care should be taken when siting this plant, as it can be easily crowded out by more aggressive species. It will grow in a lawn.

HAREBELL (*Campanula rotundifolia*)
Hardy perennial; s/p.sh. Height up to 45 cm (18 ins). Light blue flowers in summer.
Also known as 'Lady's thimble', the harebell is a native wildflower in Britain and is one of the most tolerant. Whilst thriving in most soils, it is a slender plant which could be easily shaded out in a garden, so care should be taken when choosing a suitable site.

LADY'S GLOVES (*Digitalis purpurea*)
Hardy biennial; s/p.sh/sh. Height up to 1.5 m (5 ft). Pink/purple flowers in summer.
More commonly known as foxglove, this plant will grow well in most conditions. Although it has many medicinal uses, for instance as a diuretic, it is also extremely toxic and this should be considered when planting.

Maiden pink

LADY'S MANTLE (*Alchemilla vulgaris*)
Hardy perennial; s/p.sh. Height up to 60 cm (2 ft). Lime green flowers in summer.
The common name of this plant is also applied to other varieties, such as *A. mollis*, which differs in leaf shape. The vibrant colour of the flowers and leaves make this an excellent companion plant in gardens.

ROMAN CAMOMILE (*Anthemis nobilis*)
Hardy annual; s. Height up to 45 cm (1ft 6 in). Flowers through the summer.
Dedicated to the Virgin, camomile was one of the nine sacred herbs of the Saxons. In the Middle Ages it was often strewn in the halls of castles and manors to prevent infection and improve fragrance.

MADONNA LILY (*Lilium candidum*)
Half hardy perennial; s. Height up to 1.5 m (5 ft). White flowers in summer.
This plant, a favourite of Gertrude Jekyll, should be planted on a sheltered slope which gets a lot of sun. The large white flowers are very fragrant and the plant has long been associated with Our Lady.

MAIDEN PINK (*Dianthus deltoides*)
Hardy evergreen perennial; s/p.sh. Height up to 23 cm (9 ins). Pink/red flowers throughout the summer.
This is one of the older varieties of dwarf dianthus and is excellent for growing in rock gardens. The Marian dedication of this plant, as

with the maidenhair fern, has been questioned by some experts, but unless you are a perfectionist, it remains a very attractive summer-flowering plant for a Marian garden.

MARIGOLD (*Calendula officinalis*)
Hardy annual; s. Height up to 50 cm (20 in). Flowers throughout summer. Dedicated to the Virgin, marigolds were used in medieval times as a remedy for intestinal problems, liver complaints and insect and snake bites. They were also believed to provide protection from evil influences.

THRIFT (*Armeria maritima*)
Hardy perennial; s. Height up to 13 cm (5 ins). Pink flowers in summer. This plant is a native to British coasts and is also known as 'Lady's cushion' and 'sea pink'. Owing to its native habitat the plant is extremely resilient and will grow well in most soils, providing they are well drained. It is perhaps best sited in a rock garden.

WILD STRAWBERRY (*Fragaria vesca*)
Hardy evergreen perennial; s/p.sh/sh. Height summer 25 cm (10 ins). White flowers from spring to autumn.
This plant, symbolic of purity and righteousness, provides excellent ground cover and can be planted at the front of beds or in containers. The leaves are wonderfully architectural and the fruit not only good to eat but also fragrant.

comes to tell her she will bear Christ. Or you could focus on gold or blue-coloured flowers, both colours associated with the Annunciation. Golden rod (*Solidago virgaurea*) would be especially appropriate. There is a legend that as a child of three Mary was given to the Temple in Jerusalem as a dedicated virgin. However the chief priest was divinely instructed to find her a husband from amongst the descendants of David. To do this, all the unmarried men thus descended were ordered to bring a rod to the Temple and leave it on the altar. Whichever one's rod flowered was to be Mary's husband. Another suitable feature for the Annunciation station would be a pool of water, showing Mary reflecting God's will.

Snowdrops (*Galanthus nivalis*) are associated with Candlemas in February, the festival of the purification of Mary after the birth of Jesus, and have long been planted to celebrate her life. Richard Mabey notes in his *Flora Britannica* (Sinclair-Stevenson, London, 1996) that they are particularly common on sites of ancient monasteries.

The fourth stage would take as its theme the death of Christ and Mary's share in the Passion. Flowering hawthorn trees, bitter herbs such as wormwood (*Artemisia absinthium*) or plants with sword-shaped leaves such as the yellow iris (*Iris pseudacorus*) are reminders of the Passion or of those words about Mary's heart being pierced by a sword:

Simeon blessed them and said to Mary his mother,

'You see this child: he is destined for the fall and the rising of many in Israel, destined to be a sign that is rejected – and a sword will pierce your own soul too – so that the secret thoughts of many may be laid bare.'

(LUKE 2:35)

The fifth space could focus on Mary's Assumption into Heaven. Rather than flowers or plants, an empty space, filled perhaps with a stone or wooden bench, would indicate that Mary has ascended.

Finally, leave a space for prayer to Mary as the great intercessor. A rockery captures the feeling of life's struggle on hard ground, rewarded by flowers and plants that survive by clinging to the rock, and the hope that this symbolises. Thus your garden can become a rosary and a journey through Mary's life.

4

THE ISLAMIC GARDEN

Allah has promised to Believers,
Men and women, Gardens,
Under which rivers flow,
And here they will dwell
In beautiful mansions,
In Gardens of everlasting bliss.
But the greatest bliss
Is the Good Pleasure of Allah;
That is the greatest happiness.

SURAH IX:72, THE QUR'AN

Even the most casual reading of the Qur'an reveals how important gardens are to Islam. One of the most common images of being with God is of dwelling with him in a garden. Paradise is the Eternal Garden, the reward of those who have believed.

THE NATURE OF A PARADISE GARDEN

The garden on Earth is thus literally a foretaste of Heaven, a space where human skill can combine with Divine Will and produce a place worthy of our role as vice-regents of the world, under God. Islam teaches that we are the *khalifa* of God. *Khalifa* means someone appointed by a mighty king or emperor, to rule in his stead over an area. This may sound at one level like a licence to exploit. But nothing could be further from the Islamic mind. Instead we are expected to reflect on the authority but also the mercy, love, compassion and wisdom of the One who appointed us such *khalifa*: God. Our role is to care for God's creation as tenderly as a good vice-regent cares for the people on behalf of the king or ruler. It is in this context that the garden is to be understood, for it is not just for human beings alone. A much loved saying of the Prophet Mohammed is: 'If anyone plants a tree or sows the land and people, beasts or birds eat from it, he should consider it as a charity on his part' (Bukhari and Muslim). A Muslim garden without birds, bees and insects, not to mention cats or even other small animals, is not a real garden.

The love of gardens has particular significance for a culture and faith which arose in an area of extremes, where the creation and preservation of a garden was in itself something of a miracle. When the Arabs conquered Persia in AD 637, they found themselves in an equally difficult climate and one where, as we saw in Chapter 1, the walled Paradise garden was the only realistic garden possible. The distinctive Islamic garden is really the old Persian garden continued – but given a new theological significance as a harbinger of the Heavenly Paradise.

What Islam also brought to the garden design was a love of numbers and the use of geometric design. The ban on images in the Qur'an is absolute – though this has not stopped them from emerging as Islamic empires have grown old and complacent. But traditionally Islam does forbid the depiction of any human form and indeed often any animal form. This ban on images led Islam to experiment with abstract patterns based on plants and flowers but also on geometric design. Designers created exquisite patterns, each of which has theological and philosophical significance.

One of the main additions to garden design, especially perfected by the Moghuls in India (13th to 16th century), was the octagon. The symbolism here is that of two squares overlaid to create a stylised circle. The square symbolises humanity and the circle the unity of God. In a garden, the significance of such a combination is obvious.

Islamic gardens complement and enhance the buildings to which they belong in a way quite different from the usual Western garden. Far from being an escape from the built environment of the house, mosque or palace, the Islamic garden draws out the beauty or offsets the scale of the buildings it is associated with. The classic Islamic garden fills a courtyard surrounded by low-level rooms and corridors, or abuts the high façade of a mosque or fortress. Through architectural features such as latticed arches or fretted façades, the building appears to dissolve and fragment, only to be regrouped, but in gentler lines, by the lines and shapes of the garden. At times it is hard to see where hedges and plants, shrubs and trees stop and the building takes over.

Paradise Gardens Around the World

In the heart of the heaving souq of old Damascus, you pass through a heavily fortified gateway and turn a corner to enter – well, Paradise. The noise and smells of the crowded souq disappear, to be replaced by the gentle sound of water flowing into the rectangular pond which sits off-centre in the court-

BELOW: The Patio de la Riadh, part of the Alhambra in Granada, Spain.

SYMBOLS OF PARADISE

Like the medieval garden, the Islamic garden was rich in symbolism. To create a vision of Paradise on earth, fruit trees mentioned in the Qu'ran's description of Paradise were planted, together with cypresses symbolic both of death and eternal life. Orange trees were very popular and symbolised life while Morello cherries symbolised the fruits of the soul. Grape vines were often planted

as one of the four rivers of Paradise described in the Qu'ran was of wine. The number four is of great significance in Islamic gardens, and traditionally gardens are divided into four sections divided by four channels of water. This reveals a continuity with pre-Islamic Persian beliefs that the universe was divided into four squares; at the centre was the well-spring of life. In

Mesopotamia hunting parks were divided into four sections reflecting a belief that the world was divided by four rivers. In Spain, Moorish gardens often have narrow, twisting entranceways which both symbolised the tortuous road to Paradise, and served to heighten the sense of light and beauty when the garden itself is reached. Water was extremely important in the garden, left clear to

ABOVE: A lush rose bower, typical of an Islamic-themed garden.

reflect the surrounding buildings or the sky – this symbolised the garden as a reflection of Paradise. Like the medieval garden, in Islamic gardens the rose was the flower held in highest regard. Apart from their beauty, roses were also planted to attract nightingales. Due to their plaintive song these birds were seen as a symbol of love and longing.

yard. To reach the pond, you walk through arched trellises of roses and between small trees, in a cool yet open space, where the scent of flowers and the sound of birds soothe and quieten the soul. Low hedges of box draw the eye to the shapes and lines of the garden and of the surrounding low-lying palace rooms. Areas are set aside for sitting in the shade and just enjoying the garden. The delicate arches of the building merge into arches of flowers and roses or hedges.

I have visited this garden, created in 1749, a number of times. Each time I have been welcomed by old men and young men alike who have come to sit, to chat quietly, to smoke or to just rest. The garden becomes that place of fraternity which the Qur'an sees as being the feature of Paradise.

In Europe, the greatest of the Islamic gardens is of course in the old Moorish areas of Spain, especially Cordoba and Granada. In Cordoba, one of the oldest courtyard gardens in Europe still survives. The mosque garden of the Court of Oranges dates from AD 976 and features 100 orange trees planted in rows beside water channels culminating in 19 arches which then lead into the mosque.

In Granada stands the mighty Alhambra. Here four of the original courtyard gardens still survive. The courts help to lighten the heavy military nature of the fortress, yet do so by bringing out a delicacy which might otherwise not be seen in the building. Reflecting pools and rows of bushes or trees draw out the severe lines but soften them through the colours and shapes of nature.

Today, the most complete Islamic gardens are probably those to be found in India. Of these the most famous are the gardens around the Taj Mahal, built from 1632 to 1654 as the final resting-place of the beloved wife of Shah Jahan.

Islamic gardens are of course to be found all over the Islamic world. In Iran, heartland of old Persia, many magnificent gardens remain attached to the great mosques. Sadly, the many mosques springing up in Europe, and to a lesser degree in North America, have as yet to produce even a moderately interesting garden, perhaps due to lack of funds or land. Neither does northern Europe or North America possess any significant gardens illustrating direct Islamic influence. Some of the great walled gardens of country estates from the 18th century do, however, have strong links. For example, Norton Priory walled garden in Cheshire, England, is laid out in set squares of colour, plants, arbours and tree or shrub-lined walks, similar in feel to a Paradise garden. But being wet Cheshire, there is no stream or pond as a central feature. Quite enough water falls naturally.

But this does not mean that we in the West cannot bring Islamic influences into our own gardens. Indeed, perhaps over the next decade or so, something of the formal beauty and geometric nature of Islamic gardens can contribute to the development of our varied gardening landscape. In particular, in an age of gardens which are sanctuaries, the Paradise garden has a special role to play, reminding us as we create our secluded spaces, that God is everywhere and that the Paradise garden praises Him.

Key elements in any Islamic or Paradise garden are that it is enclosed or secluded, has lines created by trees or shrubs, geometric patterns, water and roses. The rose is the Islamic and Persian flower *par excellence*. There are many legends linking roses with the Prophet Mohammed, such as the one which claims the first rose was formed by a drop of sweat from his brow. The climbing rose in particular is a feature of Islamic gardens. The formal lines and sacred geometry of the garden was offset and complemented by the wild abandon of the climbing roses, growing where they willed – beauty and order in harmony.

Not everyone can or will want to create a completely Islamic garden. However, aspects of Islamic gardening can be brought into an ordinary

> *The Paradise garden reminds us that God is everywhere; the Paradise garden praises Him.*

LEFT: *Yves Saint Laurent's garden in Marrakech. Architectural features are often as important as the garden itself in an Islamic-style garden.*

PLANTS OF THE ISLAMIC GARDEN

Trees

ALMOND (*Prunus dulcis*)
One of the fruits portrayed in Persian literature and miniatures. It is a small deciduous tree of up to 9 m (27 ft) in height, that grows wild from Syria to North Africa. It produces an attractive display of large pink flowers on bare twigs in early spring.

BAY (*Laurus nobilis*)
This small evergreen tree from the Mediterranean has aromatic dark green leaves and can grow to between 3 m and 15 m (9 and 45 ft) in height. Widely planted in the gardens of Islam for the evergreen and culinary qualities of its leaves; in spring it bears attractive clusters of yellow-green flowers.

BLACK MULBERRY (*Morus nigra*)
A small deciduous tree, sometimes reaching 15 m (45 ft) in height, bearing juicy, edible fruit throughout the summer. It has long been cultivated and probably originated in south-west Asia.

FIG (*Ficus carica*)
The fig was commonly portrayed in Persian miniatures and grown in Indian gardens; it has long been cultivated for its edible fruit and as an attractive garden shrub. It is deciduous and grows to about 9 m (27 ft). It is widely distributed in Turkey, Afghanistan and neighbouring countries.

TURKISH HAZEL (*Corylus colurna*)
A small multi-stemmed deciduous tree often no more than 6 m (18 ft) in height, from south-east Europe and Asia Minor. A relative of the common filbert (*Corylus avellana*).

JUDAS TREE (*Cercis siliquastrum*)
This deciduous eastern Mediterranean tree, typically with a low spreading habit, grows to a height of about 10 m (30 ft). Its conspicuous purple flowers have long added colour to Persian gardens, being very attractive in late spring. Masses of red-brown seed pods deck the tree in autumn and winter.

MEDITERRANEAN MEDLAR (*Crataegus azarolus*)
A small deciduous hawthorn tree, sometimes up to 9 m (27 ft) in height, native to west Asia, southern Europe and north Africa. Cultivated for its apple-flavoured haw fruit which are used in jams and liqueurs.

ST. LUCIE CHERRY (*Prunus mahaleb*)
A small white-flowering cherry tree, growing to about 9 m (27 ft). First mentioned in the 12th century by Arab botanists as a tree cultivated in their gardens; probably originating in Abyssinia and acclimatised in the gardens of Seville.

STRAWBERRY TREE (*Arbutus unedo*)
A shrub or small tree sometimes reaching 10 m (30 ft) in height, found throughout Asia Minor and into southern Europe and Ireland. Its unusual soft, red fruit add visual interest. although the fruit is edible, it is bland.

Shrubs

SUMMER DAMASK ROSE (*Rosa* × *damascena* var. *semperflorens*; syn. *R.* × *bifera*)
Rambling, climbing and shrubby roses frequently won pride of place in Persian gardens and literature. This hybrid species, cultivated in Syria by the 10th century, reached western Europe quite late, in the early 16th century. It has fragrant, large flowers, varying white to red. Its petals are used in perfume manufacture.

GRAPE VINE (*Vitis vinifera*)
See page 53.

JASMINE (*Jasminum officinale*)
Shown in paintings of Persian pavilions in the 16th century, this is a deciduous, twining shrub, up to 10 m (30 ft) in height with fragrant white flowers in the spring. It is native to the Himalayas.

LAVENDER (*Lavendula angustifolia*)
A small, intensely aromatic, purple-flowering shrub from the Mediterranean region.

MYRTLE (*Myrtus communis*; syn. *Cyrilla racimiflora*)
This evergreen shrub, used in 19th century restoration of 'The Court of the Myrtles', and possibly authentic to this part of the 14th century Alhambra garden in Spain, is a Mediterranean shrub which adds delight to the Muslim garden. Myrtle grows to a height of about 2 m (6 ft) and bears white, fragrant flowers in summer, sometimes followed by purple-black berries.

SHRUB MALLOW (*Hibiscus syriacus*)
A hardy deciduous shrub, up to 3 m (9 ft) high; cultivated for gardens in various forms, some with white flowers, others with violet flowers.

TANNER'S SUMACH (*Rhus coriaria*)
A deciduous shrub of up to 3 m (9ft) in height from the Mediterranean region.

Plants of the Islamic Garden (Cont.)

Garden Flowers

BUGLOSS (*Anchusa azura, A. officinale*)

A. azura is a perennial from North Africa, West Asia and parts of Europe; it grows to a height of 1 to 2 m (3 to 6 ft) and bears attractive violet flowers. *A. officinale* from Asia Minor and Europe is usually slightly smaller with violet, sometimes white or yellow flowers.

DAFFODIL OR NARCISSUS (*Narcissus elegans, N. tazetta*)

Shown in paintings of Persian pavilions in the 16th century, widely found in gardens throughout India and at Constantinople, these are early-flowering bulbous herbs. N. elegans from North Africa and the Mediterranean is a small plant, about 25 cm (2 ft) high, with white, green and orange shades to its flowers; various forms of N. tazetta grow wild in the Mediterranean, North Africa and Iran and bear white and yellow flowers.

ELECAMPANE (*Inula helenium*)

A tall Eurasian perennial flowering herb, sometimes up to about 3 m (9 ft) in height.

FLAX (*Linum usitatissimum, L. grandiflorum*)

A range of flax species have been grown as garden plants. These include *L. usitatissimum*, an annual that grows to about 1 m (3 ft) in height and bears blue flowers. This is the ancient cultigen, probably originating in Asia, forms of which are widely cultivated for their fibre content (linen) or the oil in their seeds (linseed). *L. grandiflorum* from North Africa grows to about 75 cm (6 ft) high and bears rose-coloured flowers with dark centres.

HOLLYHOCK (*Alcea rosea;* syn. *Althaea rosea*)

A favourite both for depiction and mentioning in Persian poetry. It probably originated in Turkey or Asia. This is a popular garden biennial or perennial, up to 2 m (6 ft) high, with white, pink, purple or sometimes pale yellow flowers.

HOUSELEEK (*Aeonium arboreum*)

A Mediterranean plant, about 2 m (6 . ft) high, with red-veined flowers in the summer.

IRIS (*Iris 'Florentina', I. foetidissima, I. germanica, I. pseudacorus*)

Mentioned in Persian literature, these are attractive flowering rhizomatous or bulbous perennial herbs. The stinking gladwin (*Iris foetidissima*) from North Africa and south-central Europe grows up to 30 to 90 cm (1 to 3 ft) high and thrives in complete shade. It displays lilac flowers in early summer and spectacular orange or scarlet seeds in late autumn. Yellow flag (*Iris pseudacorus*) which grows wild in Iran, Turkey and parts of Europe, bears bright yellow flowers and thrives at aquatic margins. *Iris germanica* bears blue, white, violet or yellow flowers and is probably of Mediterranean origin or an ancient fertile hybrid.

LARKSPUR (*Delphinium brunonianum*)

A delightful violet-flowered hardy annual garden plant from Afghanistan, usually up to about 1 m (3 ft) high.

LILIES (*Lilium ciliatum, L. ledebourii*)

White lilies have been grown in Arab gardens since at least the 12th century. These bulbous perennial herbs, about 1 m (3 ft) in height, bear large, attractive flowers. *L. ciliatum* from Turkey is a tall-growing, scented lily with ivory, cream or pale yellow petals the upper portions of which are finely spotted; the fragrant lily *L. ledebourii* from Azerbaijan and Iran displays creamy-white to yellow petals spotted with dark purple or red.

MARIGOLD (*Calendula officinalis*)

See page 72.

MARSH MALLOW (*Althaea officinalis*)

Traditionally popular in Persian gardens, this is a pink or lilac-pink flowering European perennial, growing up to 2 m (6 ft) tall.

NIGHT-SCENTED STOCK (*Matthiola longipetala*)

A small annual, usually up to about 50 cm ($1\frac{1}{2}$ ft) high, with yellow, green-white or pink petals and a strong night-time fragrance. It grows wild in South-west Asia and Greece.

TREE MALLOW (*Lavatera arborea*)

A tall biennial or perennial plant up to 3 m (9 ft) high from the Mediterranean. It bears large lilac flowers in the summer.

VIOLET (*Viola* spp.)

A range of violets, both wild and cultivated, became popular in Arab gardens by the 12th century. *Viola canina* from Europe and Asia grows about 40 cm (1 ft) high and bears blue or white flowers. Violets are excellent self-propagators and can be let loose amongst mixed shrubs or shady sections of the garden. Their flowers appear in late spring.

WALLFLOWER (*Erysimum cheiri* syn. *Cheiranthus cheiri*)
Admired for their scent and beauty, they were cultivated in Arab gardens by the 12th century. Combining dense spikes of brilliant coloured flowers with an intoxicating fragrance, this southern European plant flowers from spring to early summer and grows about 80 cm (3 ft) tall.

WHITE LUPIN (*Lupinus albifrons*)
An annual herb from the Aegean and Balkans. It grows to about 1 m (3 ft) in height, each plant bearing numerous attractive white flowers.

WHITE WATER LILY (*Nymphaea alba*)
A floating plant from North Africa and parts of Europe. It has white flowers, about 20 cm (6 in) diameter, that open diurnally.

WORMWOOD (*Artemesia absinthium*)
A perennial, about 1 m (3 ft) in height, it is grown for its pungent leaves, rather than its flowers, and was popular in Arab gardens by the 12th century.

Culinary Herbs

FENNEL (*Foeniculum vulgare*)
See page 44.

GARLIC (*Allium sativum*)
A bulbiferous plant, pungently aromatic, 25 to 100 cm (1 to 3ft) tall; long cultivated for its culinary properties. It bears white or pink flowers.

MINT (*Mentha × gracilis*)
See page 44.

THYME (*Thymus* ssp.)
See page 44.

garden. The following are just a few examples.

Geometry

This does not mean the rigid lines of borders or maniacally neat hedgerows of some gardens, but is more like the creation of mazes, so beloved of the Celts and of many ancient churches. Islam sees geometry as an expression of both the order of God and the beauty and gentleness of God.

By using geometric designs you can create a place of reflection and even transcendence. Low box hedges may be planted in octagonal patterns; trees or shrubs may reflect the four cardinal directions. A special space may be oriented, via where you plant and where you leave a vista, to a place or direction important to you, as Makkah is important to Muslims.

Channels

Islamic gardens channel water and channel you. In doing so they don't just make long lines but create places which channel the vital energy of the place, linking it to the house but directing it out into the world.

So, plant in such a way, whether it be trees, hedges or borders of flowers, that you feel energy drawn into the pathway you create and yet also reflected out. Create opening spaces in your channel which allow you to sit and see your pattern, your created channel, spread outwards. A 'green' channel of plants (in contrast to the water channel) can be created by plants which increase in size the further away from the path they are. A border of, say, 2.5–3 m (8–10 ft) on either side will give ample space for such a green channel. Here you can encompass the channel and wall – essential aspects of the Islamic Paradise garden.

Bowers

Bowers are a core feature of Islamic gardens, especially of Moghul ones. Arched bowers of roses, or trees, trailed honeysuckle or wisteria create those private spaces of which Islam is so fond. Such a bower should also help to soften the buildings near it and can be surrounded by the geometric patterns of box hedges or herb garden plots, releasing fragrant smells into the air to create the ultimate secret Paradise space in your garden.

CREATING AN ISLAMIC GARDEN

The central feature of any Islamic-style garden is of course the pool or, to be more precise, the tank. This is usually rectangular, but can be square. Flowing water is a key aspect of the garden, not just because in a dry climate water is essential, but also for its sound. The gurgling of water running at a certain pace, down a channel or over stones, produces different pitches of sound. These can be used to cut out other noises. In a garden subject to a lot of background noise, you could perhaps have your water flow run over rocks and stones and splash down into your pool or tank. In one where noise is not a factor, look to produce a gentle bubble of water which fills the air with its soothing sound.

The tank itself should contain fish as well as water plants. But Islamic gardens are not greatly concerned with colour in the pond or tank. The pond serves more as an oasis of calm and as a cooling influence than a visual highlight. In the colder northern climates, however, you may wish to bring some colour into such a pool.

The tank or pool should ideally be built with walls high and thick enough to sit upon. Dabbling your fingers in the cool waters is a must for all romantic scenes of Islamic gardens! The reason for building walls is that you should be designing your pool or tank to elongate the lines of your house, to reflect their projections so that the garden begins to be seen as an extension of the house. If you have a rocky waterfall to produce sound, position this at the opposite end to the one you will usually use to approach the pool.

Beyond the hedge, create arbours of trees and roses. Roses are best planted on the house side as they then provide a slightly wild frame through which the lines of your house are seen and softened, then picked up again in the straight hedge rows. Tree arbours should be on the opposite side from the house to form a feature to be seen from the house.

Assuming that you have good walls to enclose your garden, use wisteria or other climbing plants to cover them so that after a few years, the walls have become the garden as well. If you want to break the ground up with beds, plant tulips and narcissi to create a carpet effect. One delightful way to do this is to follow what archaeology has shown was done in the Generalife, the summer palace of Granada in Spain. Here flowerbeds for such plants as tulips and narcissi were dug below the level of the path. This allowed water from the pool or tank to drain down to them from small channels carved in the path. But more importantly from the effect perspective, when the flowers blossomed, they were then at foot level, creating the delightful impression of walking through a carpet of flowers.

CREATING AN ISLAMIC GARDEN

Islamic gardens were always enclosed, so ideally create a boundary to your garden, either with a stone or brick wall or a hedge. The central feature around which to plan an Islamic garden is the rectangular pool. Traditionally four channels lead from this to divide the garden into four sections: however if this isn't possible you could build a path to create the same effect. Remember the sound of running water was essential, so try to incorporate a fountain if you can. Around the pool plant a box hedge clipped to a height of a metre (3 ft) with openings for each of the four channels

or paths. Along your four channels or paths plant a border of roses, anemones, narcissis, Madonna lilies and violets. In each quarter of your garden plant fruit trees featured in the Qu'ran's description of Paradise. These could include the morello cherry, almonds, apples, plums and oranges. Some traditional plants will not be hardy in cool climates so you may need to adapt to suit your conditions. A scaled down version of an Islamic garden could be created by placing potted citrus trees, or pots of box clipped into spheres at regular intervals around a square pond.

Key

1. Central pool
2. Channel or path
3. Box hedge (*Buxus sempervirens*)
4. Border of roses (*Rosa foetida,
   R. moschata*), anemones, narcissis
   (*Narcissus* spp.), Madonna lilies
   (*Lilium candidum*) and violets
   (*Viola odorata*)
5. Fig tree (*Ficus carica*)
6. Mulberry (*Morus alba, M. nigra*)
7. Walnut (*Juglans regia*)
8. Cherry (*Prunus cerasus*)
9. Wall or hedge

Chapter 5

THE CHINESE
TAOIST GARDEN

An ancient Chinese saying captures the essence of Taoist gardening:

> *A garden that does not yield to hills, streams
> and ancient trees but is all the work of
> humanity cannot possibly be of interest. The
> wonder of the garden is in the use of the
> scenery, not in the creation of it.*

It is this concept of going with the flow of nature that is fundamental to Taoist gardens. The idea of formal flowerbeds or serried ranks of trees or bushes is anathema to Taoism. Instead, a Taoist garden seeks to reflect in its use of what is given by nature, the Taoist approach to all life, namely, to find for humanity, a space, place and role within the greater picture of the Tao, the Way of nature. Humanity has a very elevated role in Chinese cosmology. We are here to ensure that the two great forces of yin and yang – Heaven and Earth – are kept in balance. Humanity is the balance keeper – not the innovator, but part of the very nature of nature. Taoist gardens are an articulation of this concept.

YIN AND YANG
AND THE GARDEN

The Yellow Emperor said,

> *'The principle of Yin and Yang is the basic principle of the entire universe. It is the principle of everything in creation... Yang stands for peace and serenity. Yin stands for recklessness and turmoil. Yang stands for destruction and Yin for conservation.'*

(THE YELLOW EMPEROR'S CLASSIC OF INTERNAL MEDICINE)

Yin and yang are the two elemental forces of the Chinese view of the cosmos and of everything within it. These two forces are totally opposed to each other yet because each contains a speck of the other, neither can ever overcome the other. Their eternal struggle is what provides the dynamic of life, known as *chi*, or life energy, life breath.

Yin and yang are to be found in all forms of life, but some are predominantly yin, others predominantly yang. For example, water, cold, clouds, women, winter, the North, river valleys, vegetables and the Earth are all predominantly yin. Yang is predominant in Heaven, fire, steam, men, summer, mountains, birds, dragons and the South. Each has its destructive and its constructive aspects. Neither is seen as good or bad, good or evil. Such a dichotomy does not exist in Chinese cosmic thinking, unlike the dualism that so bedevils Western thought.

One of the best models of the interaction of yin and yang is the seasons. Autumn marks the growth of the yin power, culminating in yin dominance *par excellence* in winter. Yet at midwinter, the decline of yin is already setting in, leading towards the growing yang of spring, which reaches its fulfilment in summer. But at midsummer the seeds of the collapse of yang are already sown and the cycle moves inexorably towards autumn and the growth of yin power again.

Yin and yang are not gods or divine forces. They simply

RIGHT: Magnolia × soulangeana.

describe the way the world, the cosmos, is. Their interaction causes life to be and their struggle spurs it on. They are present in every living thing and nothing is without them. Humanity has a unique role in that we and we alone are believed to have the wisdom and skills to ensure that yin and yang are balanced. Conversely, we also have the power to disrupt the balance and bring disasters of disorder upon the world. Too much yin and the world is cold, flooded or dying. Too much yang and the world is burning, deserts spread and water disappears. Humanity needs a balance of these forces and has to help maintain or even restore this balance. Gardening thus becomes not just a pleasant activity but also an aspect of our playing our part in the cycle of cosmic harmony and balance. It becomes a fundamentally sacred responsibility.

When Western writers first started describing Chinese yin/yang gardens, they were astonished by two things. The first was the sheer size of the gardens and the amount of planning and construction that went into them. But the second was the fact that what was produced looked like a natural landscape! As already explained, Westerners of the late 17th to mid 18th century were used to formal gardens laid out on geometric lines. The organised natural-ness, the planned disorder of Chinese gardens was almost beyond their ability to describe.

This planned disorder is exactly what, at its most basic, yin and yang bring to gardening. As the Yellow Emperor said, yin and yang stand for order and chaos. A Chinese garden, especially a Taoist one, tries to capture this using yin and yang elements. Thus fundamental to a yin/yang garden is the contrast between the hard and the soft. This might be a flowing stream bending around a solid rock. It might be reedbeds blowing in the wind alongside a stone pagoda. It might be a bridge over running water. Contrast is what is sought. The most common forms of this are hill over valley, water over or against rock.

Feng Shui

Feng shui, the art of geomancy, is fundamental to yin and yang gardens. *Feng shui* means literally 'wind water' and this essentially teaches that all land-scape is alive with forces of yin and yang which must be taken into account when building anything – palace or garden. *Feng shui* determines good direc-tions and bad, and advises on the scale and colour of both buildings and plants. It guides the balancing of forces already there with those brought in by human activity. It is the methodology by which yin and yang are applied or revealed in a garden.

The Nature of the Landscape

Alongside yin and yang, the Taoist garden seeks to draw out or respond to the innate nature of the landscape, of water, of trees and of plants. This idea of an innate nature is a profoundly Taoist view, not found in Buddhism to the same extent, nor in Confucianism.

Chuang Tzu, the great 4th-century BC philosopher and wit, puts this well. He uses the model of the wild horse and its innate nature and contrasts this with the way humanity tries to improve or innovate:

> Horses have hooves so that their feet can grip on frost and snow, and hair so that they can withstand the wind and cold. They eat grass and drink water, they buck and gallop, for this is the innate nature of horses. However, when Po Lo [a famous trainer of horses in antiquity] came on the scene, he said, 'I know how to train horses.' He branded them, cut their hair and their hooves, put halters on their heads, bridled them,

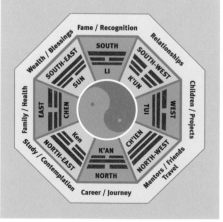

hobbled them and shut them up in stables. Out of ten horses, at least two or three die. Then he makes them hungry and thirsty, gallops them, races them, parades them, runs them together.

Replace the horses with trees, bushes, flowers, landscape or whatever else you wish from the world of gardening, and you can see what Chuang Tzu is saying. Taoists believe that the very best in nature is natural. Humanity's role is to enhance this by skill and care and by learning from nature itself – for example, by looking at how the use of nothingness or emptiness is more natural than filling everything.

In many ways, Chinese Taoist gardening is the negation of what we traditionally think of as gardening. It is a delight in and use of what is, as well as making use of what is not. This may sound like some sort of philosophical nonsense, but it is actually a practical vision of the garden. In the West we put into a garden. In Taoist gardens, it is the space between, the absence, which is as important as the presence. This is well expressed in the following verses from the *Tao Te Ching*, one of the key texts of Taoism, composed around the 4th century BC:

Thirty spokes on a cartwheel
Go towards the hub that is the centre

– but look, there is nothing at the centre
and that is precisely why it works!

If you mould a cup you have to make a hollow:
it is the emptiness within it that makes it useful.

As the *Tao Te Ching* points out, emptiness can be the very thing which defines something such as a cup. It heightens our awareness of what is around it yet it is the emptiness which makes that around it useful. The heart of a Chinese garden, but especially a Taoist garden, is empty. This emptiness may express itself in a lake or pond which provides the calm reflective centre. Look at a traditional Chinese room and you will see that it too is empty in the middle. Furniture is placed around the edges. So it is in a garden. The empty centre might be a small hill or rise, which in its simplicity forms a focal point, or it could be a space defined by bushes or trees, leaning inwards to an empty space.

A TAOIST GARDEN

This is a design for a large-scale garden. To begin with, before you start to do anything on your garden, walk it. Not just physically, but listening and seeing the flow of forces, the contrasts of the yin and yang areas or features such as shady corners, sunlit areas, high points, low points, areas which feel 'warm' others which leave you 'cold'. Feel the *chi*, the energy running through the site. It may be that certain places feel more charged than others. Look to see if what already exists has blocked the flow of *chi* around the site – something might need to be removed, cut back or reshaped to allow a free flow of energy. You need to read the landscape in the ways outlined above before you begin to think of how, to paraphrase the ancient saying quoted at the start, to 'use the scenery, not create it'.

Once you have been able to draw up a chart of the yin and yang, the *chi* and the elements already present, you can begin to plan to draw these out. This will initially include three things. First, you need to find your empty centre. It may be an undulation in the ground which can become the hub of the wheel, to quote the *Tao Te Ching*. Or it may be that you need to refocus this

CREATING A YIN/YANG GARDEN

The overall shape of a yin/yang garden should be a flowing, swirling one. As a template you could use the swirling form of a Chinese dragon as the path around your garden. Remember that contrasts form the essence of a yin/yang garden. A rockery can be a great way to embody this principle with stones, pebbles or sand contrasting with plants. As a general principle the static, inactive energy of stones embodies yin energy, while the active growth of living plants represents yang. A lovely combination would be rounded, water eroded river stones forming a background to long grasses or bamboo. Remember that colour and shape embody yin and yang. Yang colours are at the warm end of the spectrum and include red, orange, yellow and pink, while yin colours are cooler such as blue and white. Yang shapes are pointed, sharper and thrusting, while yin shapes are rounded and smoother. This means you can play with reversing the expected yin/yang pattern. For example, you could plant low-growing, round-leaved, white-flowering ground covers such as white dianthus for a yin effect beside jagged, vertically set rocks for a yang effect. These kinds of 'role reversals' remind us of the constant interaction between and integration of yin and yang. The plan opposite embodies a number of yin/yang contrasts. At the yang end of your garden plant a red-flowering azalea, rhododendron or camellia, and at the yin end a white-flowering version. A pond filled with water lilies between the two sections can act to unite yin and yang.

Key

1. Red-flowering azalea, rhododendron (*Rhododendron* spp.) or camellia (*Camellia japonica*)
2. River stones
3. Sacred bamboo (*Nandina domestica*)
4. Red, yellow or orange ground covers: mahonia (*Mahonia japonica*), ajuga (*Ajuga* spp.), sun rose (*Helianthemum*), cinquefoil (*Potentilla tabernaemontani*), geum (*Geum × borisii*), saponaria (*Saponaria ocymoides*), cranesbill (*Geranium psilostemon*)
5. Path – flag stones, occasional turf, sometimes gravel (path should be a mixture of styles)
6. Pond
7. Bridge
8. Water lilies (*Nymphaea alba*)
9. Reeds
10. Large, round boulders (moss-covered if possible)
11. Blue, white and mauve ground covers: plantain lily (*Hosta plantaginea*), aubretia (*Aubretia deltoidea*), periwinkle (*Vinca major, V. minor*), foam flower (*Tiarella cordifolia*), white dianthus
12. White-flowering azalea, rhododendron or camellia

particular piece of land. You may need to create a calm centre. This can be done through the construction of a pond, or the creation of a small hill or rise. If you do either, allow them to be natural – that is, we are not looking at a rectangular pond or a perfectly symmetrical hill.

The layout of paths in a Taoist garden is crucial. Taoism being the Way or Path, paths have a special role. In most gardens, paths are functional. They get you, the observer, around the garden either directly or in a wandering fashion. They provide access and viewing points. But a Taoist path around a garden is different. It is there to draw you into the whole. You should walk the Path of a Taoist garden not as observer, but as participant. The Path itself becomes you and you part of the Path. For example, a Path up one of the great Taoist sacred mountains leads you to encounters with myths and legends at every bend, poems carved into the living rock, meetings with flowing streams – one of the oldest images of the flow of the Tao. You are not there as observer, viewer. You are there as part of the continuous narrative of the mountain.

So it should be in a Taoist garden. The path should lead you from encounter to encounter until you reach the still nothingness of the centre, where what you find is your own self reflected back. Thus a Taoist path is not straight, but nor does it just wander in order to gain the best views. It should be of the very essence of the garden. This means that you use natural materials to create it – pebbles or stone, tramped earth if viable or grassy pathways. The path should arise from and sink back into the very garden itself. A contrast might help to make this point more clear. In a Japanese moss garden or Zen garden, the path keeps you away from the moss or raked sand to enable you to view and appreciate. In a Taoist garden, you use such materials to create the very path itself, to draw you in as participant, not spectator.

Taoist paths should always pass over water at some point or another. The water flow, as a stream or as the end of the lake or pond, should dominate the southern end of the garden as this is good *feng shui* and be complemented by a rise in the land to the North. By passing over water, especially on a path which bends and twists, even as it crosses the water, you protect yourself from evil spirits which cannot cross water, or follow bends. Quite apart from their spiritually protective role, these bridges and paths also ensure that you flow with the landscape. Don't worry if you only have a small garden and can only make a tiny bridge. It is the principle that matters. I've seen vast temple complexes in China 'protected' by a stream and bridge of minuscule proportions!

LEFT: A small garden can be very effective with a Chinese theme. A path traversing water is particularly important as this is believed to provide protection from evil forces.

PLANTS OF THE TAOIST GARDEN

Trees

APRICOT (*Prunus armeniaca*)
A small tree, up to 10 m (30 ft) tall, bearing white or pink flowers and edible, yellowish, succulent fruit.

CHINESE SCHOLAR TREE AND UMBRELLA TREE (*Sophora japonica pendula*)
The Chinese grew a number of trees associated with diligent study including the above, which is a pendulous deciduous tree to 5 m (15 ft) with white pea-like flowers in spring and attractive yellow autumn colour. Other scholar plants include Chinese parasol tree (*Sterculia plantifolia*) and various palms and bananas (*Musa* and *Basjoo*).

CHERRY, YING TAO (*Prunus pseudocerasus*)
One of the many species and varieties of oriental cherry. The Ying Tao cherry is a small Chinese tree, growing up to 5 m (15 ft) in height, and bearing white flowers in spring. *Prunus serrula* is more commonly available and very similar.

CRAB APPLE (*Malus sylvestris*)
Small tree up to 7 m (20 ft) tall bearing pink to white flowers in spring and yellow-green or red fruit in the autumn. The apple flower is symbolic of feminine beauty.

CONIFER (*Thuja orientalis* 'Rosedalis')
One of the most popular juvenile forms of the Chinese Arbor-vitae. Dwarf, with heather-like shoots. Origin unknown, but distributed by the 1920s from a nursery in Orleans, France.

MAIDENHAIR TREE (*Gingko biloba*)
This is one of the few conifers that is deciduous. In autumn its fan-shaped leaves turn yellow. It is a fast-growing tree and can reach a height of 12 m (40 ft), so it is suitable only for a large garden.

MULBERRY (*Morus nigra*)
See page 81.

MAGNOLIA (*Magnolia × loebneri*)
A small hybrid tree of garden origin, growing up to about 7 m (20 ft) tall, and bearing white or pink-tinged flowers. The flower symbolises feminine sweetness.

PEACH (*Prunus persica*)
A small tree, growing up to about 8 m (25 ft), bearing pink or white flowers and edible, yellowish, succulent fruit. Many cultivated varieties. The peach was associated with marriage and immortality.

PEAR (*Pyrus calleryana*)
A small tree rarely exceeding 4 m (12 ft). The pear is symbolic of longevity, justice and purity.

PINE (*Pinus tabuliformis*)
This species grows to 10 m (30 ft) tall and features a dense domed crown with long level branches and shoots at right angles. The pine was symbolic of endurance, longevity and reliability.

PLUM (*Prunus cerasifera*)
The plum was associated with longevity and its five petals are symbolic of the 'five clans' of China: Chinese, Mongolians, Manchus, Mohammedans and Tibetans.

POMEGRANATE (*Punica granatum*)
A deciduous Eurasian shrub, about 3 m (10 ft) tall, found wild from the Himalayas to the Mediterranean. Long cultivated in gardens world-wide for its large, reddish-orange, edible fruit. It bears showy red, bell-shaped flowers in spring and autumn leaves that may be tinted red. The pomegranate was symbolic of fertility and good luck.

WILLOW (*Salix matsudana* 'Tortuosa')
A very hardy willow this will thrive in almost any situation. The Chinese call this dragon's claw willow because of the contorted shape of its branches and shoots. It grows to 7 m (20 ft). The willow is associated with meekness.

Shrubs

INDIAN AZALEA (*Rhododendron simsii*)
An evergreen shrub with red flowers, growing up to about 3 m (9 ft) tall. It is native to southern and central China and parts of the Far East. In China it has long been valued as a garden plant; it reached Western gardens by 1812. The azalea flower is symbolic of passion.

BLACK BAMBOO (*Phyllostachys nigra*)
One of the most elegant species and varieties of bamboo in the Taoist garden. Very distinctive because of its black stems which can grow up to 3 to 10 m (9 to 30 ft) tall. Bamboo is symbolic of longevity, courage and endurance.

BLUE HYDRANGEA (*Hydrangea aspersa*)
One of several oriental hydrangea shrubs, bearing large leaves and pale blue flowers. Grows up to 4 m (12 ft) tall.

CHINA ROSE (*Rosa chinensis*)
This yellow, scented and repeat-flowering rose is one of the parents of modern roses.

MACARTNEY ROSE (*Rosa bracteata*)
A fragrant climber from China, 3 to 6 m (9 to 18 ft) tall, with white petals.

Garden Flowers

CHRYSANTHEMUM
(*Chrysanthemum indicum*)
Grows 30 cm to 1 m (2 to 3 ft) tall and bears large, pale yellow, single flowers. The flower is associated with joviality. The Chinese were great hybridisers of chrysanthemums and produced much of the gene pool used in the commercially grown flowers of today.

DAY LILY (*Hemerocallis altissima*)
A Chinese lily, growing up to 2 m (6 ft) tall, and bearing pale yellow flowers that are nocturnally fragrant.

HOLLYHOCK (*Alcea* spp.)
See page 82.

LOTUS (*Nelumbo nucifera*)
The lotus is the holiest of Chinese flowers. It symbolises rebirth and beauty. Unfortunately it is not hardy in cooler climates, but you could substitute with the pink flowered *Nymphaea*.

MOUNTAIN PEONY (*Paeonia suffruticosa*)
A tree peony from China, Tibet and Bhutan, growing up to 2 m (6 ft) tall. It bears large flowers, mainly pink to white in colour. The peony is associated with good fortune and masculine drive.

NARCISSUS (*Narcissus* spp.)
See page 82. Narcissus was symbolic of optimism.

The use of Chinese characters or even entire poems carved onto rock or wood is a special delight of Taoist sites. In most temple gardens, a large character (say about 1–1.5 m [3–5 ft] tall) will be displayed. Often this will be the character for longevity, for the garden is a symbol of the mountain where the sages seek immortality. Other favourite characters are those for good fortune or Heaven or Earth.

The use of poems is especially delightful. One of my favourite small Taoist gardens rises from and above the ancient temple of A Ma in Macao. Here there are carved poems extolling the view and the beauties of the site. The largest such carved poems must surely be the ones carved on Tai Shan, the greatest of the Taoist sacred mountains. Written by the 18th-century Emperor Chien Lung, they praise the mountain and the Emperor himself in roughly equal quantities. The carving is known as the Hundred Thousand Feet Stele.

Planting out your Taoist garden requires restraint. Chinese gardens, especially Taoist ones, are not full of flowers or arbours. They use space with the odd feature. An ancient tree will be a much loved feature, but if there is not one on site, then plant a tree which can have space to grow and achieve its natural shape and size. Pine, gingko, cypress and juniper are favourites in China and most are seen as symbols of longevity. Plant one or two trees in clear spaces in order that in years to come you or your descendants can wander here and be drawn into the natural beauty and shape of the tree.

Trees, plants and flowers almost always have some symbolism attached to them by the Chinese. This is rather delightfully expressed by the following quote from the Emperor Chien Lung (he of the earlier poems on Tai Shan):

> When I view with delight an orchid, I love to see righteousness. When I observe pines and bamboos, I recall Virtue. When I am beside a gently flowing stream, I appreciate honesty. When I see weeds, I despise falsehood. That is what is meant by the saying,
> 'The Ancients get their ideas from nature'.

Perhaps the most famous flower in a Chinese garden is the water lotus. Although its imagery is usually associated with Buddhism, where its ability to rise from the mud through the dark waters to blossom in the sunlight is likened to the soul rising from the mud of existence to nirvana, Taoist gardens love them too. They also like the imagery, though Taoism does not see this world or the body as being unworthy of the soul, as so much of Buddhism does.

As for fruit, peaches are highly prized in Taoism. They are the fruit of immortality, feature in countless legends and are associated with mighty Taoist deities such as the Queen Mother of the West. Peach trees are thus often found within Taoist gardens. Plums are also valued for their association with fertility and new life. Bamboo is ubiquitous, providing highly useful screens to divide one part of the garden from another as well as emphasising lines and verticals.

A YIN/YANG GARDEN

This can be created in almost any size of garden, though the design given here is for a medium-sized one. It works on the principle of contrasts.

For the basic design, allocate a space within which you can create swirls of colour and shapes which can meet and mingle. If you have the space, plan a path which follows the swirls so that you become part of the pattern, as if you were the movement of *chi* – energy or breath – through the garden. If space does not allow, then try to give a flowing aspect to some part of the design – perhaps construct a water course, or plant reeds or bamboo which sway in the breeze.

A yin/yang garden can be formed by combining rocks, stones or sand with plants. The rock, stones or sand constitute the yin element, the energy more static and inactive while living plants represent active yang energy. A good mixture is to have a rock as the centre of your yin section of the garden. From this stones tumble down and outwards, ending in sand as a sort of blurred edge where the yin meets and mingles with the yang. Use the rock and stones as a basis for a rockery, but try to find plants which have a dark green foliage and if possible a white flower to maintain the yin influence. If you want plants rather than rock and stone as the centrepiece, a magnolia is a splendidly Chinese plant to have. Its dark leaves and white flowers are perfect for the yin element, but keep it well pruned. A *Magnolia sieboldii* might be best, as it is easy to manage. From a central magnolia bush, again, use white-flowering plants or a variant upon this theme. Gentians are good for both the yin and yang side.

For the yang element, choose plants which combine colour – especially reds, yellows and blues – with plants which reach towards Heaven, the yang direction. For example, the heart of your yang section could be a maple such as *Acer palmatum* 'Atropurpureum' or a *Cornus alba* 'Sibirica', red-barked dogwood. The red bark and the erect stems signify the yang – male, fiery aspects. From this, fuchsias such as 'Tom Thumb' or 'Mrs Popple' are good plants to spread outwards and continue the reddish hue.

If you can provide water as the divider/unifier of the two parts, then that is splendid. Allow it to run gently between the two opposing forces. If not, then as suggested earlier, plant something which is reed-like enough to wave in the wind, thus giving the sensation of movement and energy. Bamboo would be a traditional choice.

An Indoor Yin/Yang Stone Garden

In 19th-century China, the most expensive item for any garden was a yin/yang stone. Such a stone had to be monumental – frequently up to 4 to 5 m (12–15 ft) tall. Its distinguishing feature was that it was curved, carved and riddled by waterworn holes like a worm-eaten cheese. The solidity of the rock and the holes and curves carved by water was seen as the best embodiment of yin and yang possible: the soft and the hard. A fine example could cost £10–15 million in today's terms. For an indoor garden, you can use this idea, but not on the same scale, nor costing quite so much!

> *Balance is reflected in a hard rock worn by smooth water*

The best part of this garden is finding your stone. On holiday, look in rockpools, or under waterfalls, or in stream beds. Find a stone carved into shape by water and/or wind. Find a stone which is hard but hollowed – your own yin/yang stone.

Once you have found your stone, create a trough or find a large bowl in which you can set it. A bowl is the best, for the circle shape represents Heaven, while your stone will stand for Earth. Yin and yang in the very core elements of your garden. Radiating out from the stone at the centre, plant *Soleirolia* and *Tropaeolum polyphyllum*. The former, also known as 'mind-your-own-business', has white flowers and tiny vivid green round leaves. It grows to around 5 cm (2 ins) in height and spreads rapidly, so will need controlling in any container. *Tropaeolum polyphyllum* grows to around the same height and has small bright yellow flowers and grey-green leaves. Use the diversity of colours to produce a yin side and a yang side, but also to enjoy when they cross over or climb over each other. That really reflects the inter-action between yin and yang

CHAPTER
6

JAPANESE BUDDHIST AND SHINTO GARDENS

In any other country, it would just be a bend in a winding service road, curving up a high hill from the town below to the museum above. In area it is perhaps half an acre. It could have just been left as a grassy bank, indistinguishable from any other adjunct to a roadway. But this is in Japan and therefore in this small restricted space an exquisite garden has been created. Not only that, but a tea-house as well.

From the tea-house, you look up through a haze of plum trees towards the road. Except the road is nowhere to be seen. Landscaping and the beauty of the trees have removed all trace of it. You could be in the middle of the countryside.

Here you sit, sipping tea and politely being invited to write a haiku poem on the view before you, in the grounds below the MOA museum, Atami, Japan.

THE NATURE OF JAPANESE GARDENS

The most striking thing about Japanese gardens is their compactness. They can utilise the tiniest spaces and create a sensation of wilderness, wonder, beauty and space which is almost magical. The reason for this is very simple: the vast majority of Japan is too mountainous for development, so humanity has had to carve space out in the little valleys and on the thin coastal regions where the mountains meet the seas. Space is at a premium in Japan and none of it is wasted. It is from this that the compactness of the Japanese garden springs.

The mountains shape Japanese gardens in other ways as well. Their dominance – from the great sacred volcanic cone of Mt Fuji to the Hidaka mountain range of the northern island Hokkaido – manifests itself in the gardens through the creation of miniature 'mountains' and the predominance of rock as a basic element of almost all Japanese gardens. Likewise, the waters that run from the mountains in innumerable streams, waterfalls and rivers find an echo in the role of water in the garden. In effect, a classic Japanese garden is Japan in miniature, which – given certain Japanese beliefs – means the universe in miniature.

Shinto Shrines

To understand the evolution of Japanese gardens it is best to visit an ancient Shinto shrine. Shintoism is the indigenous religion of Japan. Shamanic in origin, it shares many aspects of its belief and style with Taoism in China. Rooted in nature, it teaches that the physical world and the spiritual world co-exist. This is particularly made manifest through the *kami*. *Kami* are spirits which can be encountered through certain aspects of nature. They are not 'in' the rocks or water or trees, but can be summoned or encountered through such objects. Thus all aspects of nature have a *kami* potential. However, certain places and objects are the residence or doorway to a particular *kami*, which will be discernible to those with spiritual insight and skills.

This can be seen in the ordinary Shinto shrine in an urban area. An ancient tree, now probably standing alone in the midst of a roadway, will be the focus of a small temple. The shrine may be no more than 3.5 m (12 ft) across, but within this will be a sacred gateway, the *torii*, a wandering pathway probably set beside a small moss garden. Stone lanterns will be set at path level and the tree itself will be garlanded with a *shimenawa* (a plaited rope hung with white paper), prayer clothes or tablets. Bamboo and perhaps bushes such as an azalea *(Rhododendron* spp. Azalea Group*)* or *Camellia japonica* will give both height and depth to the tiny space, spilling out over the walls. The tiny temple, always built of wood, will have a bell or clapper to alert the *kami* to your presence. Wicker screens, wooden poles, thatch or wattle and daub enclose and screen the sacred space and give a sense of natural barriers keeping out the outside world.

A grand Shinto shrine may use a hillside as its natural setting. The pilgrim climbs the hill along a steep but bending pathway which leads through ancient woods, past vast moss-covered rocks to the central shrine. The shrine seems to emerge from the natural environment as just another part of nature.

THE ZEN GARDEN

The most famous of Japanese gardens are of course the Zen gardens. These extraordinary works of art are usually quite small, the size of a modest court yard in a temple. Their astonishing feature is the absence of what Westerners usually consider to be the elements of a garden – namely, plants, grass or water. Instead they are constructed of gravel or sand, raked to represent the movement of water, with rocks to represent islands and mosses to indicate land spread.

Yet all this is actually somewhat irrelevant, for a Zen garden is the art of minimalism applied to gardening. It is the Taoist quest for the silent empty centre taken even further. It can be seen in the magnificent minimalist ink paintings of Japan, when a few strokes of the brush summon up an incredible image, more through what is left out than by what is painted in. This is how a Zen garden works.

> *A Zen garden is the art of minimalism applied to gardening*

Zen Buddhism owes a great deal to Taoism. It emerged in the 6th century in China, where it is known as Chan. Its great founder figure is the dramatically ugly and immensely loved Bodhidharma, an Indian monk who arrived in China in the 520s, preaching that all other forms of Buddhism were meaningless because they had failed to grasp the one fundamental truth: that at the heart of everything is nothing.

To emphasis this, Chan/Zen Buddhism invented the koan, a statement which seems to be illogical but upon which the monk or lay person is called to meditate constantly until its meaninglessness or impossibility breaks down

the norms of language and meaning to reveal the emptiness and thus reality within. Famous examples of koans include 'Imagine the sound of one hand clapping' and 'If you meet the Buddha on the road, kill him.'

This exploding of the meaning of language can be traced back to the Taoist writings of Chuang Tzu and the *Tao Te Ching* of the 4th to 6th centuries BC. The Taoist denial of the reality of that which seems known is best captured in the opening lines of Chapter 1 of the *Tao Te Ching*:

The Tao that can be talked about is not the true Tao.

The name that can be named is not the eternal Name.

> *The Zen garden is an expression of the emptiness of reality.*

Zen Buddhism took this further and perfected one of the world's most astonishing philosophical and practical belief systems. Emptying yourself, you could find yourself, whether you were a warrior (for Zen Buddhism was much favoured by warriors) or a monk – or a gardener. The Zen garden thus is an expression in form of the emptiness of reality. It is meant, like a koan, to concentrate the mind and clear it of all that obscures.

Creating a Zen Garden

This should not be undertaken lightly! Zen gardens need careful management and protection. The carefully raked patterns do not create themselves and can be instantly wrecked by a playful pet. However, as a use of a small space they can be exquisite. You can even produce the same design in miniature for an indoor space, using a large window box or a bay window – a sort of bonsai Zen!

Many Zen gardens use the twin features of islands and ocean. The island is created by a rock or stone which in its natural shape evokes the shape of an island. Remember that most Japanese islands are volcanic and thus erupt upwards. Around these islands, the gravel or sand is raked to produce an ocean-like effect. The regular raking of the sand or gravel is in fact an intrinsic part of the Zen meditation process.

Alternatively, you could feature some stylised animals, for example, the rocks or stones could be a family of bears swimming or whales surfacing. Again, the gravel or sand is raked to produce the water effect.

Moss and the occasional ground plant such as creeping thyme (*Thymus vulgaris*) can bring some green to this otherwise dry and sandy landscape, but avoid anything which will flower, thus focusing attention in the wrong way.

Don't be too ambitious. A Zen garden is small and perhaps what you

LEFT: In this Japanese-style garden a path leads to a Zen garden of gravel and rock in the distance.

could most easily create is simply a Zen corner of your garden, which complements the rest. Zen gardens require almost daily care, raking the sand or gravel, weeding, clearing leaves or rubbish, etc. Be realistic about this or you could end up with just grubby sand or patchy gravel.

As with so many Japanese gardens, the Zen garden is an enclosed garden. The walls should be mellow in colour as well, for example wicker or brick. The walls are used in very different ways in different Zen gardens. Some have nothing growing upon them, though a small gingko tree or pine might be sheltered in a corner. The Ryugen-in garden at Daitoku-ji temple in Kyoto is an example of this. Others provide a framework for hedges and shrubs, as is seen in the Daisen-in garden, also in the Daitoku-ji temple, Kyoto.

While Zen gardens are the most famous of Japanese gardens, more typical are the tea-house gardens, the moss gardens, the stroll gardens and the *tsubo* – courtyard gardens.

PLANTS OF THE JAPANESE GARDEN

Trees and Dwarf Trees

CEDAR (*Cryptomeria japonica* 'Bandai-sugi')
A widely planted form of the Japanese cedar, irregularly shrubby to 2 m (6 ft). Blue-green foliage turning reddish in winter. Distributed outside of Japan after the 1930s.

Cryptomeria japonica 'Sekka-sugi' (syn. 'Cristata')
A narrow, conical form of the Japanese cedar, 6 to 8 m (18 to 24 ft) high, sometimes more. Distributed outside of Japan after about 1900.

Cryptomeria japonica 'Mankichi-sugi'
A low-growing form of the Japanese cedar with an upright habit, reaching only to 1 m (3 ft) in height.

CHERRY (*Prunus* 'Accolade')
One of the many hybrids of Japanese flowering cherries, this grows to a height of 10 m (30 ft) and bears beautiful pink flowers in early spring.

ORNAMENTAL WEEPING CHERRY (*Prunus × subhirtella* 'Pendula Rubra'; syn. *P. pendula* 'Pendula Rubra')
This beautiful tree spreads to 6–7 m (20 ft) and reaches a height of 3 to 5 m (10 to 15 ft). It features deep rose blossoms in late spring. In autumn the foliage often turns crimson and orange.

JAPANESE FIR (*Tsuga diversifolia*)
This is actually the Japanese hemlock but looks very like a fir (*Abies* spp.). The crown is nearly always a multi-stem arrangement. The orange shoot contrasts well with the brilliant white of the underside of the leaf. It will eventually grow to 10 m (30 ft) but is low growing in most conditions.

JAPANESE WHITE PINE (*Pinus parviflora*)
The Japanese grew a number of pines, but the above is the wild species from which many slower-growing garden varieties have been derived. They have a bun shape and dense canopy with

predominantly blue-green leaves. The rare slow-growing Japanese umbrella pine (*Sciadopitys verticillata*) was a prized addition in Japanese gardens.

MAGNOLIA (*Magnolia kobus*)
This tree grows to a height of 6 to 7 m (20 ft). In winter its dark branches are decorated with downy buds which blossom into creamy-white flowers in spring. A spreading tree, after 30 years it can grow as wide as it is high.

MAPLE (*Acer japonicum* 'Aureum')
In Japan this tree is known as the full-moon maple because of its broad, rounded head of yellow foliage in spring and early summer. In spring it bears purple-red flowers which give way to red-winged fruit in summer. In autumn the leaves flare into red, orange and gold. It is slow-growing, eventually reaching a height of 3 to 5 m (10 to 15 ft).

THE TEA-HOUSE GARDEN

The tea-house or tea garden is the model domestic garden. Unlike shrine gardens or stroll gardens, such gardens are designed to be homely rather than miniature landscapes of mountains and seas. If anything, they try to create the sensation of being in a secluded secret grove or hidden dip in the mountains. The shrubs and bushes for the tea garden are chosen for their 'quiet' qualities – flowering shrubs are rarely chosen. Rather, the design is one of subdued colours and a background patina of evergreens.

Narrow paths emphasise the hidden aspect of the tea garden and the use of stepping stones rather than a full path indicate a semi-wild area through which one tiptoes. Indeed, to a great extent, the tea garden is a pathway. The pathway passage is an induction area taking you from the bustle outside to the quiet contemplation of the tea-room. As such it is designed to utilise a very small space in an intense way, hence the emphasis on evergreen as a powerful but ultimately cooling background tone.

JAPANESE MAPLE (*Acer palmatum* 'Senkaki')
This maple features coral-red branches and shoots whose colour intensifies during winter. The foliage turns a warm golden-yellow in autumn. It grows to a height of 6–7 m (20 ft).

Shrubs

BAMBOO (*Arundo donax*)
A giant Mediterranean grass introduced into gardens throughout the world; stems up to 5 m (15 ft) tall, clumped. Leaf blades striped white in some forms.

KUMAZASA BAMBOO (*Sasa veitchii*)
This bamboo is one of the most popular species in cultivation in Japan. It is dwarf to about 30 cm (12 in) with white-edged leaves. It can be invasive, spreading by rhizomes. A less invasive and equally popular species is *Shibataea kumasasa* growing to .75 cm (2½ ft) with zig-zag canes.

JUNIPER (*Juniperus chinensis* 'Kaizuka')
A form of the Chinese juniper 4 m (12 ft) high or more, of upright habit, with branches spreading very gracefully. Distributed outside Japan after about 1920.

Juniperus chinensis 'Japonica'
A wide spreading, dwarf form of the Chinese juniper, occasionally conical and up to 2 m (6 ft) high.

Juniperus conferta
Mat-like Japanese shrub used as creeping ground cover.

RHODODENDRON (*Rhododendron yakushimanum*)
This compact evergreen shrub was introduced in 1934 from the mountains of the Japanese island of Yakushima. It grows to a height of 60 cm (2 ft) and 1 m (3 ft) wide. Its deep pink buds open to white blooms in May.

RHODODENDRON 'Hinomayo'
An evergreen shrub which grows to 1.5 m (4 ft). It bears soft pink flowers in late spring.

The Symbolism of Japanese Plants

Most of the popular plants of the Japanese garden are rich in symbolism. The peach tree is possibly the most important tree symbolically. It was representative of immortality, and the god of long life is often depicted holding a peach. The cherry was also extremely popular and represented spring and youth. The peony, also popular in Chinese gardens, represented love, marriage and fertility, while the water lily represented purity and truth. The jointed sections of the stems of the bamboo represented the steps along the path to enlightenment while the chrysanthemum represents long life, prosperity and contemplation.

Creating a Tea-house and Cherry or Plum Blossom Garden

This garden comes into its own in spring, but during the rest of the year offers a delightful garden where the changes of the seasons can be closely observed, because you have only one plant to watch and can thus take in all the most subtle changes of colour and shape, from the first buds of spring through the full leaf of summer to the bare branches of winter.

Ideally you should have an undulating landscape, one in which the trees are at different heights and lean in different directions. A Japanese cherry or plum garden does not consist of serried ranks of trees. The intention is to create a natural hillside look, so plant in such a way that wherever you look, you will see one or two trees overlapping each other.

The tea garden assumes a stationary position – you are sitting in your tea-room looking out. It is the classic sitting meditation garden (see Chapter 7). Therefore design the garden to present itself to you from that viewing point. Trees of different height can enhance this framing effect, so plant smaller ones in the foreground and taller ones at the back for long vistas, or taller ones at the front and smaller at the back for a sensation of great distance.

Bulbs can be planted as well, but don't allow anything to overpower the time of blossom, when you can just sit and drink in the colour.

THE MOSS GARDEN

The moss garden arose quite naturally in Kyoto, the second ancient capital of Japan (founded late 8th century), because moss grows easily and rapidly in the climate of the city. However the idea of entire gardens dominated and themed on moss is a very distinctive Japanese creation. These beautiful gardens combine moss with trees, which seem to emerge rather than grow from the moss. The mellow effect of such gardens is hard to describe, combining the vast array of greens of the moss with the lichen of the trees and stones and the green of the trees themselves. There are superb moss gardens at Saiho-ji Buddhist temple in Kyoto, Japan, and in the grounds of the Hakone Art Museum. Before visiting the Saiho-ji garden you must prepare yourself spiritually by chanting sutras.

MOSSES AND FERNS

The Japanese use a range of mosses and moss relatives in their gardens. They all prefer high humidity, plenty of water and at least partial shade. There are at least 11,000 species of moss so you can experiment until you find the one best suited to your own conditions. The fine needle-like leaves of the hairycap (*Polytrichum commune*) is a delight and are the most preferred. The fern moss (*Thuidium delicatulum*) has feather-like, delicate leaves, while the pin cushion forms dense greenish-white mounds. Broom mosses (*Dicranus* spp.) and cord moss (*Funaria hygrometrica*) are both attractive and tough

Ferns enjoy the same conditions as mosses. The Japanese traditionally used several species the most notable being lady fern (*Athyrium felix-femina*), Japanese pointed fern (*A. goeringianum*) and Japanese shield fern (*Dryopteris erythrosora*). In addition, the striking non-invasive Japanese mare's tail (*Equisetum hyemale* var. *affine*) can be grown. This has dead straight dark green leafless stems to 75 cm (2¹/₂ ft in) in tight clumps, spreading slowly using short rhizomes.

RIGHT The beautiful moss garden at Ryoan-ji temple, Japan.

A MOSS GARDEN

Key
1. House
2. Miniature pines or junipers (see plant list pages 106–107)
3. Flag stone path
4. Boulders
5. Miniature pines or junipers
6. Stone lantern
7. Wisteria (*Wisteria sinensis*)
8. Stucco wall
9. Bamboo (*Arundo donax*) and trees
10. Bamboo screening

Remember both shade and moisture is essential for a moss garden. Choose a section of your garden shaded by the house, a fence or wall, or mature trees. You can encourage moss to grow over stones by smearing the stone with yoghurt and covering it with plastic wrap. The following plan can be reduced in scale to suit a section of a garden. Undulating ground over which your carpet of moss flows is crucial so you will need to be prepared to create a series of small rises. Plant a group of two or three small trees such as miniature pines or junipers at the edge of the first rise (1.5m [5 or 6 ft]) above the level of the garden. On the left hand side build another gentle rise. Create here the effect of a small mountain stream valley by placing rocks along the sides of a curving channel. Encourage moss to grow over the rocks to give a sense of timelessness. You can also plant further miniature pines along the channel. Moving to the right hand side of the garden create a smaller rise and place a stone lantern here on the side of the rise that faces the house. The far wall of the garden closes the space. Ideally it should be covered with outdoor plaster or stucco and painted a pale grey, pale rose or light earth colour. Just off the centre of the wall plant a clump of bamboo or a tree such as *Acer capillipes* to provide a strong vertical element. You can also train a wisteria to climb along the wall. It is also important to adapt any other walls to suit your garden. Screen a larch fence or brick wall with bamboo screening or plant a hedge of *Prunus cerasifera* 'Nigra' or hornbeam (*Carpinus betulus*).

Creating a Moss Garden

While often difficult, this is not impossible. Again, it can be done on a large, medium or indoor level. Remember that moss is a plant as much as a tree is. It has roots and leaves and therefore needs nutrients, water and light as any other plant does.

The key features of a moss garden are undulation and trees. Your space needs to provide a moving landscape over which the moss seems to pour like a slow-moving carpet and trees around which the moss movement gently swirls.

Decide whether you are going to view the garden from one place or wander through it. If you are viewing from one place, plan an undulating aspect from this point. If your garden is to be one to stroll around, plant your paths in such a way that they are as discreet as possible. Stepping stones are ideal for this, with the occasional larger stones to provide standing and viewing points.

For such a walking garden, start with a dip again, but fill it with small trees to screen the rest of the garden and to give the sensation of being in the woods almost the moment you set out. The path can then meander around a similar landscape to the one described in the landscape plan left, except that you might wish to use the two rises to intensify the sense of going into a small stream valley with your path wandering along the bottom of it. Furthermore, the channel should run diagonally but in waves across the bulk of the site, affording you shifting views of the two rises, the trees and shrubs and the 'stream valley'.

An indoor moss garden is logistically a much more straight-forward project. Follow the same principles of an undulating landscape, but substitute bonsai for the trees and pebbles for your boulders and rocks.

THE STROLL GARDEN

The stroll garden is a larger-scale non-religious garden. As the name indicates, these gardens were designed for walking around and for observing the views. They arose in the Edo period of Japanese history (1600–1867). The powerful nobles who built them were able to exploit much larger sites than those of the usual Japanese garden. Stroll gardens are masterpieces of precision and of design, utilising the shapes and flow of the landscape but transforming it. Views and vistas were deliberately created to evoke past glories and to replicate famous scenes. So vast were some of these gardens that they swallowed up farms and farmland, which were sometimes left to add a pastoral dimension to the garden.

Much of the inspiration for the design of stroll gardens came from China and the best known gardens re-create places or views in China, such as the famous dike in the Western Lake of Hangzhou, reproduced in the stroll garden of Yosui-en, Wakayama.

The stroll garden comes very close to the classic country estate garden or park of the 18th-century English landscape.

THE *TSUBO* OR COURTYARD GARDEN

The *tsubo* or courtyard garden is perhaps the art of gardening – rather than the art of Zen gardening – at its finest in Japan. The *tsubo* is the world, the cosmos in microcosm. The *tsubo* garden started life as the garden in small courtyards in palaces or grand houses. Today it is to be found in the grounds of hotels and inns, beside office premises and in private homes. Though a tiny garden, through layers of shape and style it gives the impression of a world within a world.

Sometimes this is done by taking just one plant and using it to create the dominant feel of a garden, supported as ever by the evergreen shrubs as backdrop and depth. Wisteria, for example, is very popular for this. In other gardens, ponds, rockeries, elevated pathways, bamboo screens or wicker fences, potted plants for height and strategically positioned stone lanterns give a depth and almost confusion of images and impressions which fill the small area and seem to expand outwards and inwards in such a way as to make space explode.

Yet again, such gardens rarely use bright coloured plants or flowers, pre-ferring to go for depth of colour. The only time they explode into colour is in autumn, or in spring if they have cherry or plum blossom.

A simple water feature consisting of a bamboo pipe dripping water into a bowl can also form the basis of a *tsubo* garden. The bowl should ideally be set into moss or a bed of pebbles with bamboo or tall grasses providing extra height. Try marram grass (*Ammophila arenaria*) or tufted hair grass (*Deschampsia cespitosa*). Sedge is also useful. If space permits, greater tussock sedge (*Carex paniculata*) is delightful for its ability to shoot up and spill outwards.

RIGHT A simple water feature consisting of a bamboo water spout, granite bowl and pebbles can become the focal point of an oriental-style garden.

7

GARDENS FOR
REFLECTION

'Gardens for reflection' sounds like a contradiction in terms to
some gardeners! Time to reflect in a garden – with all those weeds,
all that trimming and cutting? Yet many gardeners find that that
is exactly what does happen in a garden. Just the simple rhythm
of a garden, the different tasks at each time of the year, offers a
time for reflection. In a world where we can find any food we
want at any time of the year, our sense of the rhythm of the
seasons has almost gone. But the garden reminds us of the truth
expressed in the Bible,

> *There is a season for everything, a time for*
> *every occupation under heaven. A time for*
> *dying, a time for planting, a time for*
> *uprooting what has been planted.*

(ECCLESIASTES 3:1–2)

The seasons also bring their own kind of reflection. Spring brings
the joy of new life, linked inextricably with the Resurrection in
Christianity. Summer brings fruitfulness and fulfilment, as well as
the need to prune in order to prevent the more vulnerable from

being overwhelmed by the more exuberant. Autumn brings intimations of mortality; that, in a strange way, deeply satisfying sense of loss and decay which you know in six months will have sown the seeds for new life. Winter brings harshness and the cold and presents the gardener with the apparently dead world when the bare bones of the garden lie open to view and one can only really take stock of what is. A garden for reflection can enhance the natural meditative aspects of a garden.

Any garden can be a garden of reflection. A flower or plant which you were given by someone dear or which a loved one especially cherishes, can evoke their presence or memory. A shrub or tree or some specific feature like a pond or rockery may have been created at a particular time and may give you cause to reflect on the joys and troubles of that period – now all in perspective. A lawn where children play, the quiet corner where beloved pets sleep, all this and more is to be found in every loved garden. But there is also a place for both public and private gardens created deliberately to aid and stimulate meditation.

In one sense, a garden for reflection exists wherever a garden has been lovingly created. In my garden, for example, there is a tree planted for our neighbours across the road to see. They lost a dear friend and the tree is there to blossom around the time she died and to be a reminder in the most positive way, of her life and spirit. In this chapter, however, we go beyond that. We are looking at the deliberate creation of a garden designed to aid and assist deeper reflection, to enable people to focus in a way which an ordinary garden usually cannot.

ELEMENTS OF A GARDEN FOR REFLECTION

The Way

In both Christianity and Taoism, the spiritual way is often described as a Path. Indeed the word 'Tao' from which Taoism comes means to walk a path, the path or Way of Nature. Jesus said: 'I am the Way, the Truth and the Life' (John 14:7), while in the *Tao Te Ching* it is written:

> '*A ruler who walks the Way*
> *Is like a river reaching the sea*
> *Gathering the waters of the streams*
> *into himself*
> *as he goes.*'

Both faiths often talk about life being a journey in which the journey is

RIGHT: In a garden of reflection a gateway can signify the border between the material world and an area of tranquillity and spirituality.

more significant than the arrival. Look at your garden path or the routes around or across your garden. These can be turned into something more than just a convenient way to and from one place or another. They can become flowing Ways, Paths that do more than just traverse the garden. For example, allowing the land to dictate the flow of a path. A sharply inclined garden can of course be dealt with by steps. But what about a meandering path which allows you to flow with the inclination of the land?

Seating

Where to sit is important. A garden of reflection means taking time, allowing yourself to stop, rest, think, listen, smell, even taste what is around you. 'Natural' seats such as large rocks, tree trunks, raised grassy knolls are perfect, though my son loved to stretch out on our old brick wall and read quietly. More conventional seating – benches, for example – need to seem right and natural. If you are really ambitious, try a medieval turf seat. (See Chapter 2.)

Materials and Colours

Think about what to make the garden features such as the path from – wood blocks or rough rock slabs perhaps. A gravel path allows small creeping plants to colonise its edges. Fringe your path with flowers – forget-me-nots, daisies, crocuses for the spring. Plant them and bend the path to accommodate them. Look along your path and find spaces for colour and shape – a block of irises to break the flow or a magnolia to spill out over the path. Build terraces, breaks or paths with old bricks mellowed by wind and sun. A flat piece of land which has no shape or hidden corners can be turned into a journey of encounters by constructing mounds and dug out dips through and between which a path can wander. Use a rock as a break in the flow or pattern –something stark and uncompromising. This allows different views and hidden perspectives which would never appear in a flat garden with a straight path down it. A garden for reflection calls for reflection upon the garden first.

Think carefully about which flowers you wish to incorporate. You may wish to aim for a traditional English flower garden, as developed in the 19th century. This is perhaps best exemplified as being a garden overwhelmed by flowers which appear to be in a 'natural' state of profusion, but which are in fact very carefully planted and planned. The gardens of Gertrude Jekyll perhaps best exemplify this style of garden (see pages 131-132).

Colour is crucial. Think about mellow colours, colours that will be sustained for much of the year. For trees, look for barks that give variety – a silver birch (*Betula pendula*) with its irregular bark and colour; an evergreen such as a pine, for example, Scots pine (*Pinus sylvestris*), or a juniper bush (*Juniperus communis*). Perhaps if you have the space and want to leave a monument of your life which could live for 2,500 years you could plant a fine redwood tree with its extraordinary depth of colour and textured bark.

On a more modest level, you could use ivy, such as a *Hedera canariensis* with its creamy variegated leaves, or the *Hedera helix* 'Oro di Bogliasco' with its golden spots – hence its common name 'goldheart ivy'. The shapes, colour and spread of ivy, clothing a wall, climbing a dead tree or hiding something like a garage or garden shed, brings a sense of reflection. Ivy also has a remarkable deadening effect on noise, which is important in a garden for reflection.

Shrubs such as the *Skimmia japonica* 'Foremanii' provide wonderful, full shapes, a richness of leaf colour and the glory of their flowers. Holly bushes (*Ilex*) and berberis also offer shape, year-round colour and that dash of brilliance which is their berries.

As a place of quiet reflection, a pool is almost without parallel.

Centres of Calm

Still spaces of reflection are important and stone or water can provide these. The reflective image of the pond has long been used as a symbol of the reflective nature of the mind. When the water is stilled, the reflection of all around is perfect – as the reflection of the Taj Mahal in India is perfect in its reflecting pool. But when the surface of the pool is disturbed, then it is like a disturbed mind, unclear, just showing broken images. As a place of quiet reflection, a pool is almost without parallel.

A stone or rock can play a similar role – a stone which draws the eye and then allows the mind to reflect upon and from it; a rock which expresses the vastness of evolution and which brings the worries of the present into a wider, more cosmic perspective. In my study I have several stones, many of which are fossils but some of which are just stones of great beauty which I use to calm my mind and to draw me back to earth. Their incredible age and the fact that they will still exist when I am long gone, help me keep things in perspective. Combine pond and stone and you are well on your way to a reflective garden.

Moss Gardens and Rockeries

Moss gardens or rockeries can be excellent as gardens of reflection. The time and patience needed for a moss garden aids reflection, while the selection of appropriate rocks and plants, and the need to construct a habitat for them, brings reflection on the struggle and beauty of life. See Chapter 6 for a guide to Japanese moss gardens.

Gateways, Statues and Mazes

Give your reflective garden purely human touches which nature cannot provide, for both you as an individual and the creativity of our species are part of nature and evolution.

An example of this might be a gateway. A gateway marks the boundary between worlds. The lich gate of a churchyard, for example, marks the boundary between the physical and the spiritual and was the place where coffin bearers would traditionally rest. 'Lich' is an old English word meaning 'corpse'. The Moongate of China and Japan marks the boundary between the public area of a garden and the enclosed secret area. A gateway, wooden perhaps, or metal, or even made of a yew hedge or by two arching trees, can signal to the visitor that he or she is entering a special, a sacred space.

Likewise, the introduction of a statue can enhance the sense of another Presence, the sense of humanity and creativity reaching outwards. One of my favourite sculpture gardens is at Dartington Hall in Devon, where statues and abstract sculpture made of diverse materials draw you on and around like magnets of reflection.

Another intriguing feature would be a labyrinth. In Europe, the circle labyrinth design is one of the oldest known and is found carved on neolithic monuments. To create a labyrinth may sound over-ambitious. But labyrinths can be very temporary. An arrangement of stones on a courtyard, a mown pattern in a grass lawn or meadow, a pattern of potted plants – all these offer the means

RIGHT: Autumn leaves can provide a beautiful focus for reflection and contemplation.

of creating a labyrinth. And the nature of a labyrinth is that of a mandala. The pattern leads you inward in a journey of mind and soul. The intricacies, the need for direction, for a sense of where this is leading you to, all these are symbols of the spiritual journey of life.

A SEASONAL REFLECTIVE GARDEN

Perhaps the simplest and in many ways the most satisfying of reflective gardens is the seasonal garden. We all want a garden which will offer colour, variety and diverse stimuli to the senses, throughout the year. In selecting plants, shrubs or trees for such a garden, look to create as diverse a garden as possible. You may want to theme it or you might pick up on the Walking Meditation Garden described at the end of this chapter. Maybe you can use it to reflect your understanding of the garden as sanctuary, providing habitats for wildlife and looking to see whether your 'sanctuary' is where you escape the wider world or draw strength to go back into that world and make a difference.

Finding beautiful plants for spring, summer and autumn is not a problem. Winter, however, is the most difficult time for gardens, for whilst there is still much to do, in terms of pruning and preparation for spring, there is little to show for it. Many people make the mistake of attempting to plant for winter colour and, whilst this is possible, it is often better to look at plants for their structure and foliage, not simply their flowers. Many trees, silver birch (*Betula pendula*) for example, look almost at their best in the winter as one is able to fully appreciate the beautiful bark and fine branches.

The following are some suggestions for both themes and plants for a seasonal garden:

Spring	New life, resurrection, rebirth, recovery
Summer	Fullness, abundance, fecundity, energy, life
Autumn	Maturity, decline, decay, mellowness
Winter	Death, restraint, hardness, survival, but also Christmas, Hannukah and New Year – festivals of hope born in the midst of apparent death and decay.

PLANTS FOR EVERY SEASON

Spring-flowering Plants

CEANOTHUS (*Ceanothus impressus*)

A stunning evergreen shrub with a vast number of bright blue flowers in late spring and early summer, ceanothus looks especially effective with plants such as *Clematis montana* trailing through it.

DUTCH CROCUS (*Crocus vernus*)

As with bluebells or snowdrops, crocuses are particularly effective when grown within a lawn or under trees in semi-shade. Grown from corms, they come in a huge range of colours from white through to vibrant yellow or purple and can add a splash of colour to the cold spring mornings. An attractive alternative is the *Crocus angustifolius*, or 'cloth of gold', which has bright yellow flowers and orange stigmas.

DAFFODILS (*Narcissus* spp.)

This genus of plants is probably the most synonymous with springtime, with its bright yellow, white and orange trumpet-shaped flowers looking particularly effective when planted in drifts. There are many cultivars of this genus, with flowers that are single, double or triple, and the choice is a matter of personal taste. My favourite is the bright yellow *Narcissus pseudonarcissus*, or 'wild daffodil', a species which is smaller than most of the cultivars but is beautiful in its simplicity.

ENGLISH BLUEBELL (*Hyacinthoides non-scripta*)

Approximately 25 cm (10 ins) in height with pendulous trumpet-shaped bright blue flowers in spring. They are relatively easily self-spreading and will thrive in

Foxglove

semi-shade in most soils. Their natural habitat is woodland and so they grow well under trees.

SPANISH BLUEBELL (*Hyacinthoides hispanica*)

A similar plant of about the same height but perhaps more upright in habit. The flowers are a slightly more vibrant blue and they are easier to grow than *H. non-scripta*. However, if these are to be incorporated into a wildflower garden, then ensure that you get the English bluebell.

FORSYTHIA (*Forsythia suspensa*)

This is a beautiful shrub which likes a sunny position and which grows in most fertile soils. It originated in Japan and has brilliant yellow flowers in spring. The flowers do not last long but provide a vivid splash of colour for a number of weeks.

Other good spring plants are bulbs such as tulips. The bulbs give new growth early in the year and their new shoots bursting through the cold ground early in the year are a symbol of hope and regeneration.

Summer-flowering Plants

CORNFLOWER (*Centaurea cyanus*)

One of the oldest and best-loved annuals, cornflowers are easy to grow and reach a height of 60 to 90 cm (2 to 3 ft). The intense blue flowers make a beautiful focus for reflection and contemplation. *Centaurea moschata* has larger scented flowers in a softer colour range.

GERANIUM (*Geranium × magnificum*)

True geraniums, or cranesbills, are hardy plants which provide excellent ground cover and attractive symmetrical flowers throughout summer. The less hardy pelargoniums are commonly called geraniums owing to a similar leaf shape but have irregular flowers. It is the pelargonium that we often see used as a bedding plant and in hanging baskets. This particular geranium has large deeply cut leaves and violet-blue flowers in midsummer. It provides an excellent edge for borders and grows to around half a metre (2 ft) in height.

IRIS (*Iris sibirica*)

This popular plant has stunning blue flowers in late spring and early summer. Irises grow well in most soils and are effective when mixed with tulips and other long-stemmed plants.

MARGUERITE (*Argyranthemum frutescens*)

Originally thought to be a chrysanthemum, this pretty and easily grown shrub is now considered a separate genus. *A. frutescens* has attractive daisy-shaped flowers throughout the summer. White flowers are most common but yellow and pink varieties are also available. The foliage is an unusual grey-green colour and looks very effective in drifts in a border or grown as a standard in containers.

POTENTILLA (*Potentilla fruticosa*)

This is a beautiful tall deciduous shrub that will grow to around a metre (3 ft) in height. In summer it has masses of flowers which vary in colour from white to vibrant orange. 'Abbotswood' has attractive white flowers in summer.

Potentilla

Hydrangea

Autumn-flowering Woody Shrubs

BUDDLEIA (*Buddleja davidii*)

Also known as 'the butterfly bush', this can be one of the most attractive shrubs in the garden. Although it is a native of China it flourishes in the UK in particular in almost any soil. The plant has beautiful mauve flowers in late summer and early autumn which are borne at the end of long arching canes. These canes can look straggly if not pruned back hard and late winter is the best time for this. It can grow up to around 4 m (13 ft) high.

HYDRANGEA (*Hydrangea paniculata*)

This deciduous shrub, also a native of China, has large white flowers that appear in late summer and turn purple as they age. Whilst it flourishes in many countries it does need a moist fertile soil and the flowers benefit from the shade, as they are prone to scorch in full sun. The flowers appear in late summer and finish in the autumn. After flowering the shrub should be pruned; this is best done in late winter to encourage larger flower-heads. This plant can grow to 3 m (10 ft) in height.

MAHONIA (*Mahonia japonica*)

This fragrant shrub is perhaps best suited to a larger garden as it can grow to be 2 m (6½ ft) tall with a spread of up to 3 m (10 ft). The delicate sprays of yellow flowers are borne from autumn to spring. It flourishes in partial shade with a moist fertile soil and is perhaps best situated amongst other shrubs as it needs little management such as pruning.

PINEAPPLE-SCENTED SAGE (*Salvia elegans*)

This is one of the many hundreds of members of the *Salvia* genus. As the name suggests, the foliage has the scent and taste of pineapple, and the plant produces small red flowers in late summer and autumn. It is a most attractive plant which is hardy and can grow very tall. The foliage is a vivid green colour.

SAXIFRAGE (*Saxifraga fortunei*)

A pretty plant which looks excellent at the front of borders or in gravel paths. It has masses of small white flowers in autumn and is very frost hardy but will not tolerate dry conditions.

Dwarf Winter Plants

ACANTHUS (*Acanthus spinosus*)
This plant is a native of the Mediterranean which will grow well in most rich, well-drained soils and is frost tolerant. The flowers are white in colour, contrasting with the purple bracts, and are borne on tall (1.2 m [4 ft]) spikes in summer. However, as with the globe thistle (see right), the flowers are not the only reason for planting this perennial. The leaves are deep green and glossy and are divided into segments. As each is tipped with a spine, these are not the most welcoming of plants to garden with, but they are certainly one of the most striking.

Christmas rose

CHRISTMAS ROSE (*Helleborus niger*)
This attractive evergreen perennial produces greenish-white flowers in winter. It grows to around 30 cm (12 ins) in height and needs partial shade in a rich well-drained soil, regular moisture and the occasional application of manure.

DWARF YEW (*Taxus baccata* 'Dovastonii Aurea')
This unusual form of yew is a slow-growing conifer with horizontal branches and golden foliage. As with most yews, it benefits from an alkaline soil and is very hardy. Its spreading habit make it good for ground cover and it is particularly effective when planted in larger rock gardens or on the edges of lawns.

GLOBE THISTLE (*Echinops ritro*)
This plant was a favourite of Gertrude Jekyll, not only for its blue flowers and flowerheads borne in summer but also for its beautifully shaped grey/blue leaves which she often combined with lavender. The plant is a perennial and benefits from being cut back to ground level in late autumn. It will grow to a height of over a metre (4 ft) in most well-drained soils and thrives in full sun.

HAKONECHLOA (*Hakonechloa macra* 'Aureloa')
This beautiful variegated grass originates from Japan and has narrow leaves of yellow and dark green. It is very hardy and thrives in either full sun or partial shade in most damp, fertile soils. This perennial will grow up to 60 cm (24 ins) in height and will provide good ground cover in a bed or will stand alone in a container.

JAPANESE HOLLY (*Ilex crenata* 'Golden Gem')
Although this variety of holly rarely flowers it does have small yellow-green leaves and black berries. It usually grows to around 2 m (7 ft) in height and requires deep soil for its roots. It is compact with small leaves and benefits from gentle pruning in spring.

OPLISMENUS (*Oplismenus africanus* 'Variegatus')
This evergreen perennial grass has white and green striped leaves with a pink tinge. Grasses are usually planted for their architectural qualities and this is one of the best. A native of the tropics, it is often damaged by frosts and may require additional protection through the toughest winter conditions. It will grow in any moist soil and will reach up to around 30 cm (12 ins) in height and up to 2 metres (6 ½ ft) in spread.

SAVIN JUNIPER (*Juniperus sabina*)
This evergreen shrub with black berries is extremely hardy and grows to 1–3 m (3–10 ft) in height and up to 4 m (13 ft) in spread, although this can be controlled through pruning. It is an attractive spreading shrub with reddish bark and deep green leaves and will tolerate any well-drained soil.

TANACETUM (*Tanacetum haradjanii*)
This is a dense mat-forming evergreen perennial which has beautiful silvery-grey leaves. Although its yellow flowers are borne in summer, the leaves are wonderful throughout the year. This is a quick-growing plant and needs to be cut back regularly, but it will provide good ground cover. It will grow to around 38 cm (15 ins) in height and spread in most well-drained soils. It is not suitable for a sensory garden (see Chapter 8), as it is poisonous.

AN ALCOVE GARDEN

Even if you have no garden whatsoever, you can still create a reflective garden. For a reflective interior garden, find a room which is quiet and feels comfortable. Once you have chosen such a room, find the right space within it. An alcove is best, but any part of the room with a curve, bend or indentation will do. Here you are going to create space and simplicity, so you will need to clear everything out of the way. Choose a subdued, perhaps single colour background.

Into this space you are going to introduce just three or four things to create your garden. First of all, find something natural to use as a base, for example, a flat stone, a bowl filled with water or a wooden block. This introduces a basic element into your space.

Now you need to find a picture or a symbol or carving that you want to use as the focus of your meditation. This could be a painting you especially love, a symbol you associate with faith, such as a cross or a Qur'an, a prayer wheel or a statue of a Hindu deity – whatever brings you to reflect on the purpose behind life. Even better, though, is something abstract, something like a written word or Chinese character, a broken pot or some fragment. Such abstract material, urging us to reflect on the unknown or incomplete, can be very powerful. This object needs to take centre space on the wall, above the natural object you are going to use as a stand. Now you are ready to add the last two items.

The first is a plant which will fill the left or right-hand side of your space, helping to define it but not dominate it. This could be a pot plant such as a fern (for example an adiantum such as *Adiantum pedatum*, North American maidenhair fern, which grows to about half a metre [2 ft]), a tropical plant such as a yucca or, for the appropriate season, a bulb producing tall stems and flowers such as a gladioli or a hyacinth. The intention here is to have a plant which emphasises the height of the space you are creating.

Finally, you need a small plant to stand on the stone, wood or water support. For water, either a small water lily or a water hyacinth can thrive well in a small bowl of water which is 'fed' regularly or which contains soil at the bottom. For wood or stone, a small plant such as a pansy or miniature rose can be very suitable.

You now have the elements of your reflective garden. They are simplicity, a natural element to earth you, a reflective object to draw you out, a splash of colour and strength to one side, holding your eye within the space and providing a boundary to your reflection garden, and finally, a flower or plant which in its delicate smallness and fragility reminds you of yourself.

Such a garden is best viewed from floor level. Find a comfortable old cushion or pillow and sit on that. Allow yourself to join in, in whatever way is best, with the natural and humanly constructed elements of your garden. Just a few minutes a day calmly sitting and allowing yourself to be drawn into the images can be remarkably restful and possibly even occasionally enlightening.

For an outdoor alcove garden, think in terms of a sitting meditation or reflective garden.

A SITTING MEDITATION GARDEN

This builds upon the alcove idea discussed above. Unless you have the means to afford sweeping vistas, perhaps complete with a purpose-built folly on a hilltop miles away, as in 18th-century landscape gardening, you are looking at the use of a small space, a space which can do one of two things: draw you in, focusing upon a detail – a statue, a small reflective pond, an old tree stump – or draw you through to a bigger picture, via an arched bower of flowers or shrubs through which you frame the garden and environment beyond, or via a circular space where you move from the enclosed to the open. The key is that everything should come together and make sense when you sit in the chosen spot.

Remember to try to ensure use of a sympathetic material to sit on. Stone is fine, but cold! If you hope to sit a while, make the central seating area comfortable.

Around you create either an outdoor alcove garden (see above) or the enclosed space, framed perhaps with trellises or walls, shrubs or hedges, leading to an open vista, either above such walls or through them. Scale is all-important here in that use of trees or tall plants can accentuate or diminish the sense of distance and perspective.

A sitting meditation garden may need signs of life and death. One of my favourite spring sitting meditation gardens has as its key feature a long dead hawthorn tree which is covered with clematis, in particular *Clematis alpina* or *Clematis montana*, giving a cascade of flowers. Death and life – what a meditational theme!

LEFT: *A place for contemplation is essential for a truly meditative garden.*

Or you could take significant Christian plants (see Chapter 3) and build around them. In Chinese sitting meditation gardens, the focus is on the fusion of shape – circles, squares – with water and straight lines such as bamboo. The greatest of all sitting meditation gardens are of course the Zen stone gardens of Japan (see Chapter 6).

A WALKING MEDITATION GARDEN

This can be created in any space so long as you have sufficient room to move around and create visual breaks. This can be done by trellises over which climbing roses, clematis or other such climbers can grow, hedges, a small clump of trees or, if you have the space, landscaping with mounds and dips. The idea is to create quiet secret corners, places which you 'happen upon'.

Decide what the feature or theme of your walking meditation garden will be. Features can be a reflective pond – in which case plan somewhere to sit – or a mossy bank, wooden bench or old tree stump. It could be a statue or a cross – if so, again provide yourself with a place to sit or lie from which to see this feature. Perhaps frame it with bushes or a hedge, or have paths radiate out from it. Should it be elevated? If so, the mound could be a rockery or a grassy meadow-style mound, sown with wildflowers such as the common spotted orchid (*Dactylorhiza fuchsii*), the common field poppy (*Papaver rhoeas*) and the primrose (*Primula vulgaris*). Should it be in a dip? If so, ferns and other plants which enjoy darker, wetter terrain could create a sense of nature and sculpture arising from the earth.

Choose plants for the whole year. Plan to walk your garden in every season. See pages 122–124 for a list of suitable plants for each season. Make the garden rich in colour. Marian gardens (see Chapter 3) also offer a form of meditational garden.

But perhaps for many, a really important part of a walking meditation garden is that you can walk barefoot in summer, touching the ground. You can lie in the sun and look up through the branches to the sky, or at night, with senses aflame, gaze at the stars.

A WALKING MEDITATION GARDEN

A wonderful basic structure for a walking meditation garden is a spiral. Following the design opposite you walk into your spiral along one path, and exit along another. Look for a neglected or enclosed corner in your garden. A wall or fence will form a nook which you can make more private still by planting screening shrubs such as camellias or rhododendrons. This will help block noise and give the sense of entering a special and discreet place. Border your spiral with two low hedges; lavender or box would be delightful as they will release a scent as you brush past. There are a number of options for the path; you could lay a gravel path which can be meditatively raked as you walk in the tradition of the Zen garden. Or you could make the path itself the garden. For example, between flag stones you could plant bulbs, mosses and low-growing ground cover so that your path becomes a meditational journey through the seasons. Give some thought to what to place at the centre of your spiral. A water feature such as a fountain or simply a large ceramic bowl lined with beautiful stones could make a wonderful meditation focus.

Key

1. Flag stones
2. Screening shrubs: camellias (*Camellia japonica*), rhododendrons (*Rhododendron* spp.)
3. Hedge: lavender (*Lavandula angustifolia*) or box (*Buxus sempervirens*)
4. Spring bulbs: daffodils (*Narcissus* spp.), grape hyacinths (*Muscari* spp.), tulips (*Tulipa* spp.)
5. Ground cover: alyssum (*Lobularia maritima*)
6. Wall or fence
7. Water bowl

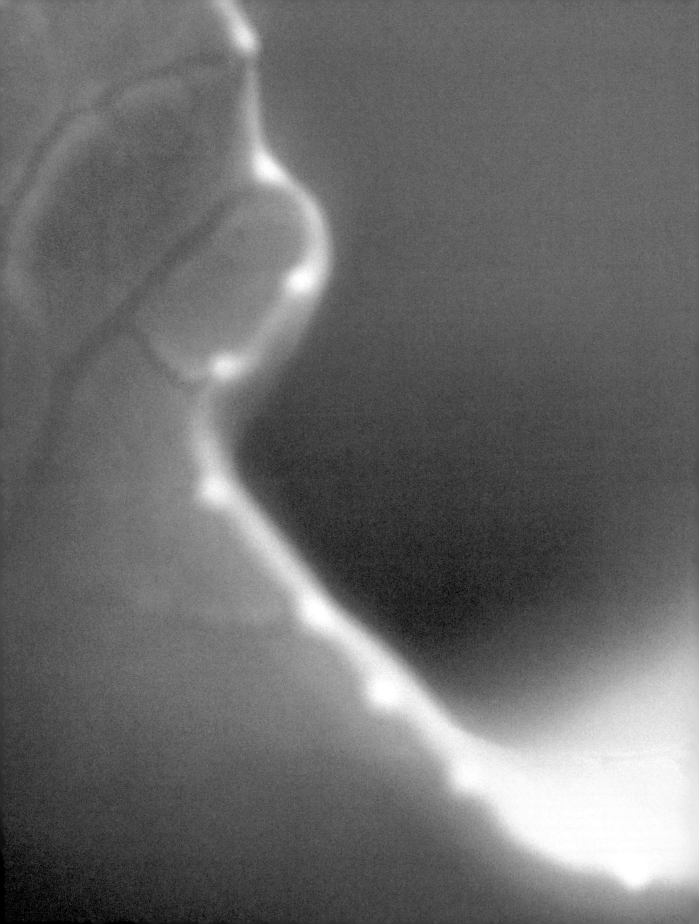

THE SENSORY GARDEN

A sensory garden combines reflection with sensation. In a sensory garden we celebrate the beauty of nature focusing on the delight of colour, smell, texture and sound. It is a different aspect of the sacred, but important nonetheless. The sensory garden recognises the sacred in the very essence of nature.

Colours, smells, textures and sounds combine to create a powerful ambience and it can be said that if these elements are not in harmony then the garden as an entity has failed. The great garden designers such as Gertrude Jekyll and Capability Brown were masters of this art and their designs show this in very different ways. Brown's 18th-century landscapes, which incorporated great lakes and trees, provided a tame wilderness where people could stroll around the grounds in complete safety and feel the wind blowing through the trees and listen to the sound of water. The reasons that Brown's designs were so successful was that in mimicking the physical patterns of nature he had also incorporated the peace of the wilderness without the danger.

Gertrude Jekyll was an expert at this on a smaller scale. Though her designs are perhaps most famous for the use of herbaceous borders and planting in drifts of colour, her work went far deeper than that and by using her superb knowledge of plants she was

able to create within tiny areas both riots of colour and havens of peace for meditation. She was, perhaps, at her best when teamed up with the architect Edwin Lutyens whom she met in 1889, and the result of this astonishingly successful partnership can be seen in Munstead Wood, Surrey, Jekyll's home for many years.

The garden at Munstead Wood is probably the finest example of Jekyll's work. Around each turn of the straight gravel paths is something different and as such the garden is truly an assault on the senses. Jekyll shows off her range of abilities in this garden for within a matter of metres you are taken through beautiful lawns, shrubberies, rock gardens and through to the woods which surround the garden. A colourful herbaceous border suddenly ends and you are standing in the peaceful dappled shade of the nut walk. The paths leading into the woods are important, as they show the intrinsic influence of the natural countryside on Jekyll's design work. Her garden at Munstead becomes more formal the further one goes away from the woods.

Incorporating different experiences for the senses into a garden benefits everybody who visits it. The following are a few ideas for a sensory garden.

SOUND

Every religion has recognised the sacred aspect of sound: from chanting to choral singing sound has become a means to transcend the everyday. In a sensory garden you can focus on the sounds of nature to create a sense of peace and harmony.

For many people an important first step is to block out external noise. You can use various methods of both hard and soft landscaping to achieve this. Many sounds, such as the noise of traffic, building sites and sometimes even other people, are often unwelcome in a garden and plants and trees are much more effective at blocking this out than walls or fences. In addition to this the leaves on a tree also filter out many airborne pollutants. Naturally deciduous shrubs and trees lose much of their effectiveness in autumn and winter, however, so many people opt for coniferous hedging plants such as the infamous Leyland cypress, × *Cupressocyparis leylandii*, which was introduced into Britain as a faster growing and considerably less attractive alternative to yew. In terms of deciduous hedging plants, beech (*Fagus sylvatica*) or hornbeam (*Carpinus betulus*) are very popular. Even after the leaves have turned they

remain on the plant, providing a golden brown hedge through the autumn and winter which rustles beautifully in the wind. In choosing a plant for blocking out noise a basic rule of thumb is the more dense the plant is in terms of its foliage, the more effective it will be.

Once you have reduced unwelcome noise, you can begin to explore how to introduce calming and inspirational sounds. It is possible to do this through imported man-made features such as wind chimes and water fountains. Running water, such as a fountain, provides a relaxing aural focal point.

Water constantly varies in the sound effect produced. Explore the different sounds of water running over stone, or splashing into a basin from a greater height. You can also use the sound of running water to dull out or block off traffic and other background noise. Wind chimes of either metal or wood, such as bamboo, can introduce music into a garden.

Plants themselves make wonderful sounds. The rustle of foliage of trees and of plants and grasses can be a magical feature, especially when mixed with birdsong and the humming of insects such as bees. Perhaps the best for this are the grasses, sedges and bamboos. Good examples include frosted curls (sedge) (*Carex albida),* golden bamboo (*Phyllostachys aurea),* tufted fescue (grass) (*Festuca amethystina).*

> *The rustle of foliage of trees, shrubs and grasses can be a magical feature.*

Whilst sedges and grasses do not grow high or dense enough to block out noise on a large scale, bamboos may well do so. In their native China many of these plants can grow to over 6 or 7 m (around 20 ft) and can be very invasive, but the smaller examples, such as *Phyllostachys aurea,* will not grow to be quite this large and can be confined and planted in limited spaces such as containers.

Other natural ways of encouraging sound into a garden is by planting for wildlife such as insects and birds. By following the broad ecological principle that the greater the number of insects and other food sources such as berries, the greater the number of birds, it is possible to create a haven for wildlife in a garden by simply planting the appropriate plants. Meadow plants, as already mentioned, are excellent for encouraging insects, while plants such as limes (*Tilia* spp.) are extremely attractive and also provide water and extra food in the winter to help the native species.

SMELL

The use of incense in religious ritual and ceremony works powerfully to heighten all the senses and focus the participants on the sanctity of what is taking place. You can achieve similar effects in your own garden. Flowers and shrubs that are heavily scented, such as lily of the valley, stock, jasmine and honeysuckle, should be separated slightly so that the smells of each one might be fully appreciated. Seasonal smells could be considered; see pages 140–141.

A camomile lawn can be a wonderful sensory experience. The fragrance of the plants is released when walked upon. If a solid path is necessary in your

AROMATIC PLANTS

The most obvious group of plants for strong smells are the herbs such as rosemary, sage, lavender and lemon balm. These should be planted at the front of beds where people can touch them.

Aromatic Herbs
ANGELICA (*Angelica archangelica*)
This is an ancient biennial herb which self-sows regularly. Its medicinal properties are widely recorded and it is used today, although mainly for cooking, in France. It has attractive leaves and will grow in any soil in a partially shaded site. At maximum height it grows to between 1 and 2 m (3 to 6 ft).

BEE BALM (*Monarda didyma*)
This annual plant grows to just over a metre (3 ft) in sandy soil. Its leaves, when crushed, give off a citrus smell and the plant carries white or pink flowers in the late summer. It was not grown in monastic herb gardens, as its native country is America.

SOUTHERNWOOD (*Artemisia abrotanum*)
Southernwood's highly aromatic leaves were traditionally used as an insect repellent and as a nosegay to protect against contagion. It grows to 1.5 m (5ft) in height.

LEMONGRASS (*Cymbopogon citratus*)
This grass, which gives a potent lemon smell if crushed, is a native of India and therefore often cannot survive colder winters. It is often

best to treat it like an annual and replant every year in the spring once the worst of the frosts are over. Lemongrass needs a fertile soil that is light and well drained and it can grow to about 1.5 m (5 ft) in height.

LESSER CATMINT (*Calamintha nepeta*)
This compact little annual grows in most partially shaded conditions in any soil. In many ways it resembles catmint, hence the name, but, as with bee balm, it is not a native to Europe and therefore would probably not have been found in monastic gardens. It is a hardy little plant that grows to under a metre (3 ft) in height. Its white flowers are borne in summer.

garden, then plant herbs in between the paving materials to provide the same effect. Evening plants such as nicotiana and honeysuckle make the night a wonderful time to walk in your perfumed garden.

TOUCH

In Christian tradition the laying on of hands – the power of touch – is powerfully associated with healing and the Divine. In your sensory garden celebrate this most essential of the senses and include different textures within the planting scheme. The bark or catkins of different trees such as hazel, willow, silver birch and plane can be touched and cherished, while plants with unusual foliage such as astilbes, cineraria and *Fatsia japonica* can provide useful architectural features in a bed, as can small-leaved box, eucalyptus, grasses and junipers.

There are a number of plants with unusual foliage, many of which have already been mentioned for their shapely properties, although plants with spiny leaves or thorns are obviously unsuitable. Plants that are toxic should also be omitted from sensory gardens, as this immediately limits the sensory range by excluding the possibility of taste.

UNUSUAL FOLIAGE PLANTS

DILL (*Anethum graveolens*)
This is a fragrant annual plant with
fine feathery leaves that grows up to
3 m (10 ft) in height. It will grow in
any humus-rich soil in full sun and
has yellow flowers in summer.

HAIRY GOLDEN ASTER:
(*Heterotheca villosa*)
A perennial native of America with
hairy green leaves and yellow flowers
in late summer and autumn, this
grows best in full sun in dry sandy
soil and is fairly frost tolerant.

HART'S TONGUE FERN:
(*Asplenium scolopendrium*)
Found in damp woodland, this plant
grows best in moist rich soil in
partial shade. It grows up to 60 cm
(2 ft) in height with beautiful long
green undivided fronds. It is fully
frost hardy.

LAMB'S EARS (*Stachys byzantina*)
Also known as 'lamb's tails', this
perennial is extremely good ground
cover. The silver-grey leaves are
covered in white hairs – hence the
name – and were once used medicinally. This plant thrives in fertile,
moist soil in full sun.

MALE FERN (*Dryopteris
filix-mas*)
A native of Britain, this plant's needs
are similar to those of the hart's
tongue fern (see above). This
particular fern is deciduous with
delicate pinnate fronds. It is larger
than *Asplenium scolopendrium*,
growing to around a metre (3 ft) in
height.

*RIGHT: The soft, tactile leaves of
Stachys Byzantina.*

PUSSY WILLOW (*Salix caprea*)
Although this deciduous shrub or
tree is famous for its female catkins
that are coated in silver hairs, its
leaves also have a wonderful feel to
them. It is a dense shrub with ovate
leaves and will grow in most moist
soils, preferring partial shade.

Flowerheads

In a sensory garden it is not only
plants with unusual-feeling foliage
that are important. There is also
something very satisfying about the
feel of flowerheads, especially the
larger, heavier ones. Being able to
hold the flowers is particularly
important for people with sight
disabilities.

Some examples of plants with
large flowerheads are:

AZALEA (*Rhododendron occi-
dentale*)
This deciduous azalea has white or
pink flowers and the familiar waxy-
looking leaves. The flowers can grow
to be around 10 cm (4 ins) in
diameter and, as with most of the
rhododendrons, the plant needs
acidic well-drained soil.

COMMON IRIS (*Iris germanica*)
One of the most attractive of plants,
this frost-hardy perennial has purple-
blue flowers in spring and summer
and benefits from a sunny position.
It can grow to be just over a metre
(3 ft) in height.

HYDRANGEA (*Hydrangea
aspera*)
See page 123

DAHLIA (*Dahlia variabilis*)
The Collerette group of dahlias have large single flowers with an inner collar of smaller petals sometimes contrasting in colour with the outer ones. The stems are up to 60 cm (2 ft) tall.

TREE PEONY (*Paeonia suffruticosa*)
A deciduous shrub which has large white or pink flowers in the spring. Grows well in full sun in most damp soils.

TULIP (*Tulipa sylvestris*)
A smaller tulip, growing up to 30 cm (12 ins) with large yellow flowers in spring, this particular variety is scented and prefers an alkaline soil and sunny aspect.

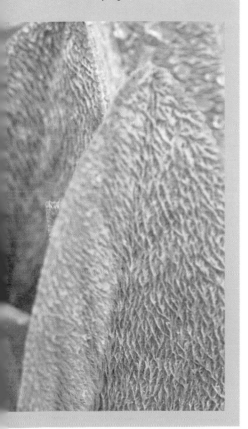

TASTE

Every religious tradition recognises food as an essential part of the sacred experience. Consider the fast and then feast of Ramadan, or the centrality of communion in the Christian tradition. The sensory garden can be a celebration of the sense of taste in the same way monastic gardens recognised the importance and sacred aspects of culinary plants.

From the immediate pleasure of rubbing chives to making your own mint tea and eating your own jam, eat your garden!

The great variety of culinary herbs offers a wide range of tastes and many also have interesting scents, such as mint, chives and onion. Herbs such as thyme, sweet cicely and lovage, rue and parsley all offer a safe adventure of taste. The inclusion of fruit such as strawberry and prunus trees will all add to this aspect of the sensory garden.

SIGHT

Sight may seem the most obvious of the senses to explore in your garden, but do think about the sacred aspects of colour. For example, a white flower garden beautifully encapsulates concepts of purity and innocence. For a meditation area think about calming flower colours of blue and lavender, but for inspiration you might choose colourful golden or yellow flowers and foliage. For Chinese gardens a yin/yang planting scheme of blue/lavender flowers with red/yellow flowers (see Chapter 5) will embody this important principle.

Blocks of colour are better than intermingled colours because they make a greater visual impact. Through planting suitable trees, shrubs and flowers, encourage wildlife, butterflies and birds, so often a joy to see. Brightly coloured stone set into concrete paths provides another interesting visual feature.

Finally, walk your garden. This may seem trite advice, but I am always surprised at how differently I see my garden when I stroll or show it to friends. Approach your garden as a wonder, as a place little known to you, and see it, smell it, touch it afresh. For what is often a daily burden of care for a garden needs to be brought back to the vision and joy it really is.

Experience your garden afresh, and in the joy of its assault on your senses, experience the joy of transcendence.

WATER – THE SENSUOUS GARDEN FEATURE

Water has long had sacred significance. In the Christian and Muslim traditions water represented the four rivers that spring from the Tree of Life in the Garden of Eden, and in virtually every faith water symbolises the life force itself. Water has been celebrated for the spiritual dimension it brings to the garden, either through sound, or the ethereal aspect of light shining through water. Over the centuries different styles of gardens have explored the properties of water in dramatically different ways.

In the Moorish Patio de la Acequia at the Generalife in Granada, Spain, a series of simple yet elegant jets of water play into a shallow channel creating a tinkling sound and the visual effect of a curtain or veil. In the Italian Renaissance garden, dramatic and technologically advanced fountains celebrated the triumph of man over nature, echoing the predominant religious view of God presiding over a rational, ordered world. For example, at the Villa d'Este, near Rome, the Owl Fountain is formed by a group of carved birds that 'sing' as a result of changes in water pressure, while the Dragon Fountain spurts powerful jets of water high into the air to represent the dragon's breath.

However, water can be effective even in the smallest suburban garden. You can create a soothing pebble pool with a wide ceramic bowl, some pebbles and a simple pump. Place the pump inside a tank made from a bucket or small dustbin. Place the tank inside your bowl and cover it with pebbles. Water will be pumped up into the air and then gently trickle back down over the pebbles creating a deeply relaxing sound. For a more distinctive sound you could incorporate a Japanese *sozu* in your garden. The sozu is a length of hollow bamboo supported by a feed pipe and placed over a small bowl or tank. The bamboo gradually fills with water until it tips forward, emptying the water. It then swings back into place, striking the feed pipe with a resonant sound.

PLANTS THAT ATTRACT BUTTERFLIES

BUDDLEIA (*Buddleja davidii*) There are many cultivars of this buddleia, such as 'Cardinal', 'Empire Blue' and 'White Profusion', all of which make a change from the original mauve-flowered form of this shrub. All of these are headily scented and are attractive to insects such as butterflies. They will grow to around 4 m (13 ft) in height in most soils. The flowers appear in summer and bloom through to mid to late autumn.

Other plants include:

BROOM (*Cytisus scoparius*)

BUDDLEIA (*Buddleja davidii*)

COTONEASTER (*Cotoneaster horizontalis*)

FLOWERING CURRANT: (*Ribes sanguineum*)

GORSE (*Ulex europaeus*)

LAVENDER (*Lavendula angustifolia*)

LILAC (*Syringa vulgaris*)

VIBURNUM (*Viburnum lanata*)

WEIGELA (*Weigela florida*)

LEFT: *Buddleia 'Dartmoor' not only looks beautiful and has a wonderful fragrance – the blossoms also attract butterflies into your garden.*

PLANTS FOR COLOUR AND FRAGRANCE

Spring

BIRD CHERRY (*Prunus padus*)
This deciduous tree grows up to 15 m (50 ft)
in height and has very fragrant white flowers
on spiked clusters in the spring. It is fully
frost hardy and its leaves can turn a vibrant
yellow in the autumn.

DAPHNE (*Daphne blagayana*)
This lovely flowering shrub with its heady
fragrance grows to 12 cm (6 in) in height
but spreads to 90 cm (3 ft). It produces dense
heads of creamy-white blooms and prefers a
shady position. *D. Collina* produces red-
purple flowers in late spring, early summer
but needs a sunny position.

VIRGINIAN STOCK (*Malcolmia
maritima*)
This hardy annual has lovely old-fashioned
sweetly scented blooms. Growing to 20 cm
(8 in) high the cross-shaped blooms come in
a range of colours from white, pink, red,
lavender and purple.

WOOD GARLIC – RANSOMS (*Allium
ursinum*)
This pungent plant is often found in
woodland. It produces white flowers in
spring which last through to summer.
Naturally, as the name suggests, it smells of
garlic, especially when the leaves are crushed
or on a warm spring day. It will grow well in
most gardens, although it may become
invasive if left unmanaged.

Summer

LILAC (*Syringa vulgaris*)
A strongly scented shrub with mauve or
white flowers appearing in summer. This
plant will grow well in most soils in sun or
partial shade and benefits from pruning
following the flowering period.

MOUNT ETNA BROOM (*Genista
aetnensis*)
This twiggy shrub reaching to 5 m (15 ft) in
height is covered in a cloud of golden-
yellow, delicately scented flowers in summer.

SWEET PEA (*Lathyrus odoratus*)
The richly scented flowers of this popular
climbing plant will bloom well into autumn.
They can reach a height of 4 m (7 ft) in
well-manured soil.

ROSE (*Rosa* spp.)
In terms of scents that evoke summer, that of
the rose is surely one of the most provoca-
tive. There are literally hundreds of varieties
and they come in all sorts of shapes, sizes and
colours. A few of the most fragrant ones
which require the least maintenance are:
Rosa × alba ('Great Maiden's Blush')
Double pink flowers and blue-grey leaves.
Rosa alba 'Semi-plena'
Pure white flowers in summer; a very old
variety.
Rosa damascena var. *semperflorens* (Quatre
Saisons)
Repeat flowering pink double blooms.
Rosa × forrestiana
Crimson flowers, tolerant of both shade and
poor soil.

Autumn and Winter

These seasons are always difficult for a
garden, but there are a few plants that will
provide that splash of colour and scent at this
gloomy time of year.

CHINESE WITCH HAZEL (*Hamamelis
mollis*)
This upright shrub grows up to around 4 m
(13 ft) in height and benefits from a sunny
aspect and an acidic soil. The yellow flowers
are sweetly scented and stay right through till
late winter. Pruning should take place in
spring.

CHERRY PIE (*Heliotropium ×hybridum*)

These evergreen plants to 60 cm (2 ft) bloom from spring to autumn. The heavy fragrance, small purple flowers and deep-purplish green velvety leaves of 'Royal Marine' make the plant a wonderful inclusion in a sensory garden.

WINTER SWEET (*Chimonanthus praecox*)

Although this shrub may not produce flowers for seven years and is vulnerable to frost, in a good year the winter-flowering, lime-yellow flowers will transform the shrub and provide an exquisite scent. It reaches 3 m (10 ft).

VIBURNUM (*Viburnum grandiflorum f. foetens*)

This deciduous shrub has deep green oval leaves and produces clusters of white flowers which appear in midwinter. It grows to around 2 m (6 ft) in height in rich moist soil and is fully frost hardy.

FIRS, PINES AND CYPRESSES

The aromas of these trees are as evocative of winter as roses are of summer. Most of them have aromatic foliage when crushed, are frost hardy and will grow in most soils. When choosing one, perhaps the most important issue is that of space. Fortunately they range from the enormous *Abies grandis* (giant fir, over 30 m [100 ft] tall) to the slightly more manageable *Cupressus macrocarpa* (9 m [30ft]). There are also the dwarf conifers, such as *Pinus sylvestris*, 'Gold Coin', which is a very attractive golden colour.

LEFT: *Here, plum 'Victoria' provides a rich sensory experience – the fruit is beautiful to look at, sensuous to touch, delicious to taste.*

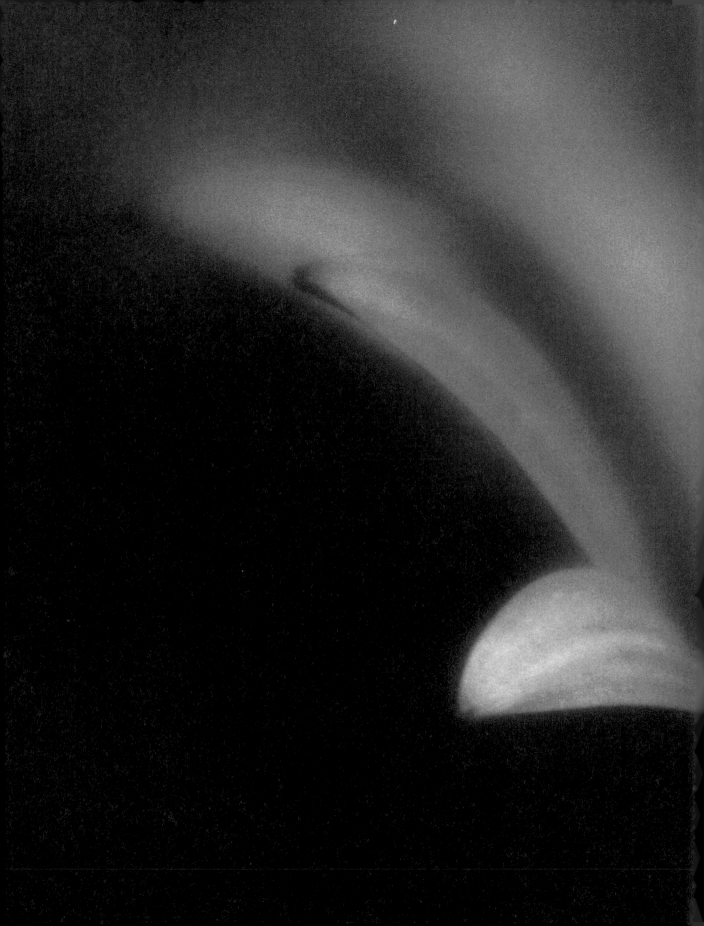

9

SACRED URBAN SPACE

Although you may not realise it, open spaces and public spaces are also part of your potential gardening influence! There are many types of open spaces over which you as, perhaps, a parent, worker, club member, local resident, or churchgoer, can have and perhaps should have an influence.

A sacred garden can simply be the right and proper use of what we have been given to love and cherish, not waste and abuse. In using open spaces sacredly, we can begin to express this wider vision, unattached to any specific sacred building or even religious tradition. However, religious traditions do offer us starting-points.

For example, the Hindu vision is of all life being caught up in the cycle of reincarnation. Nothing is either more or less than the other aspects of creation, sparks of God's love, part of the very essence of God.

With such world views, such faith, nowhere is without God or the Divine. Thus all the world, all creation is sacred or has a sacred potential which, if the Orthodox Christian teaching is followed, can be brought to fullness through humanity acting as a blessing. Perhaps it is in the very areas we have ignored, blighted or simply poorly cared for that we must look to exercise our most creative role as 'simply yet gloriously the means for the expression of creation in its fullness'.

The Sacred in Open Spaces

I first realised the power of even the smallest attempt to bring a garden into the most insignificant places when I was in Japan one year. I had been taken to a small restaurant in a very ordinary back street in downtown Atami. As it was cold I had rushed inside from the car. But after the meal, we had to wait outside for a few minutes while the car was brought round. It was then that I noticed the garden. I was standing in the car parking zone in the front of the restaurant. In any Western context it would have been an insignificant space. Perhaps a potted shrub would have stood beside the door, nothing more. Yet out of this small concrete functional space, in total no bigger than three parking spaces, had erupted a tiny garden. It brought a sense of blessing, of humanity as simply yet gloriously working wonders with God's creation. The garden consisted only of a wooden pipe with water dripping from it into a pottery fish bowl with three goldfish, set into a moss base. Surrounding this were bamboos and moss. But it gave an amazing feel to an area which was to all intents and purposes just waste space.

Schoolyards

Even the smallest garden can bring a sense of blessing, of humanity working wonders with God's creation

An urban space with an obvious functional role is the schoolyard. It can be a football ground or playground. But increasingly it is also staff car park, dumping ground and waste land. For children who love to rush around, open spaces or tarmac playgrounds are fine. But many children want somewhere quiet to talk with their friends, to hide when the going gets rough or to be still when life at home or at school bears down upon them too heavily for their years. Yet how many schools provide a garden or a quiet space, landscaped to avoid ball games or rushing to and fro?

In 1984 the World Wildlife Fund in Britain published a book, *Worlds of Difference*, on how the different religions view and treat the natural environment in the light of their creation stories and beliefs. It is still in print and is in nine different languages. This is a success in its own right. But what none of us who worked on this project expected was one of the main outcomes: the book is used primarily by Religious Education or Personal and Social Education teachers in Europe. From

ABOVE: A window box featuring tropaeolum, lobelia, pelargonium, hedera, petunia and chrysanthemum.

looking at the very practical environmental and landscaping insights gained by studying such faiths as Taoism, Aboriginal Australians, Hinduism or Christianity, the idea arose simultaneously in many minds of creating a 'sacred space' in the school grounds. Drawing upon different traditions, teachers in over 500 schools in the last decade or so have created sacred spaces, quiet gardens, in the school grounds where children can both help in making a space beautiful and find a place of calm and quiet.

This can be done very simply, by marking off an area perhaps a quarter the size of a tennis court with a simple wall or with banks of earth. The design within this enclosed space varies enormously. For some, a pond or central feature such as a sculpture or rock works. For others it might be a garden designed by the children. Others have undertaken more demanding projects. Taking the Chinese *feng shui* tradition (see Chapter 5) or the Australian Aboriginal Dreamtime idea, they have looked at the existing landscape surrounding the whole school and tried to imagine what tales it tells of ancestral creatures who fought, loved, dwelt here and left imprints in the land, as Dreamtime tales tell, or of dragons, tigers and yin and yang forces which exist within the land itself, as in Chinese belief. Then they have worked on certain areas to enhance the 'natural story' they have detected within the landscape, maybe creating a small garden area or artwork or models of the creatures they have detected. Such storyline explorations may not have very long-lasting effects on a large landscape such as school playing fields, but the idea that land can be seen, experienced and designed in radically different ways lasts a lifetime.

Some Ideas for a Sacred School Garden

There are obviously different guidelines to be considered when creating such a garden. For example the plants must be non-toxic, without thorns or sharp leaves and very hardy, and their height would need to be thought about very carefully. Although the area needs to be kept quiet and separate to achieve the desired effect, it still needs to be sufficiently open to discourage bullying and to allow teachers to keep an eye on the children using it. Often even a small hedge only 30cm (1 ft) or so high is enough to separate an area using plants such as lavender or rosemary.

The garden also needs to be fun and so looking beyond the planting scheme is important. Try thinking about an interactive yet safe garden. Instead of a bed of flowers or shrubs, have an area with a number of thick logs cut to different lengths and set into the ground as upright cylinders for the children to climb on or sit on. Garden centres and builders' yards supply stone or concrete spheres of different sizes and a series of these painted different colours makes an unusual feature.

In these areas planting schemes should be in colours conducive to peace and quiet, so whites, blues, lavenders and purples are ideal.

The amount of maintenance that the garden will receive should also be taken into consideration. Ground cover in beds will be important, as this prevents weeds from coming through.

FACTORY LAND

Around every factory or workplace there is some public land and this can be quite considerable. It can include roof space as well as ground-floor level sites. Yet how few such open spaces are ever used well or imaginatively. Car parking and pedestrian footpaths are about the limit in most cities. But with care, thought and a little money, such spaces can be made more imaginative, more sacred in their own way.

One of my favourite examples of this is a garden in Manchester, England, set between three hideous 1960–70s banking and office buildings. The three buildings soar above a consequently dark open space, hemming it in and intimidating it. The area is paved and dead. But above the entrance to the boiler room, set into the fourth side of the square, is a rooftop garden. For years it has struggled with neglect. Being over 4.5 m (15 ft) above the level of the square, little has been visible other than dark ivy spilling rather sinisterly over the walls. Then one day I spotted the top of a cherry tree. Over the years this tree has grown, almost unnoticed by the building's occupants. The appalling design of the square means winds roar through it, throwing rubbish over the scurrying pedestrians. This has caused the tree to lean as it has grown. Now, some 20 years on, it pokes out of the roof garden at a jaunty angle, a splash of colour when blooming and an alternative to the rigidity and bareness of the buildings, even in winter.

RIGHT: Planting wind-tolerant and dry-tolerant species means that any space, even a New York rooftop, can be transformed into sacred space.

CAR PARKS

Probably one of the most ubiquitous of modern open spaces is the car park. Fortunately, its blighting influence is slowly being resisted. It is encouraging to note, for example, that the British Museum is to ban cars from the forecourt, allowing that magnificent open space to be returned to its intended grandeur.

There are various ways in which a car park can be made less of an eyesore and more of an open space. Use of sympathetic materials such as blocks which allow grass to grow through the middle can help. But so can landscaping. The creation of banks of earth to hide the cars and topping the banks with trees or shrubs can help. Certainly the planting of trees as breaks between the parking spaces is an improvement. But the main problem with a car park is simply the amount of wasted space. If the strips between the rows and around the whole site are landscaped this can provide at least some small relief from the presence of the car.

This is not necessarily 'sacred gardening' as such! But perhaps if we can be imaginative and creative about something as functional and usually ugly as a car park we can begin to recapture something of the religious vision that all the world is of God and should be loved and cared for in that light. Car parks are, I would argue, a major test of that conviction!

ROUNDABOUTS

I am always struck and delighted by the imaginative gardeners who take over roundabouts in the middle of road complexes. From North America through Britain to Budapest I have seen such delightful gardens created in these open spaces – open spaces which could be just barren and functional but which have been used to create beauty in the midst of motorway and car madness.

One of my favourite examples is a sort of noble protest against the crassness of development. On the road between Ruthin and Denbigh in North Wales there is a very elongated roundabout which creates an extremely large traffic island. Trapped in this is a small cottage, resolutely lived in, with a magnificent garden spilling out in all directions.

PILGRIMAGE PATHS

One traditional sacred open space is the pilgrimage path. Europe in particular is criss-crossed by such ancient pathways, even though many have been lost over the centuries. Famous ones such as the route from southern France to Santiago de Compostela in northern Spain are still walked by thousands each year. In Wales, the Saints' Way from just west of Caernarfon to Bardsey Island is still a living route. Yet others are being re-invented, rediscovered or created, such as the routes to Canterbury or the new interfaith pilgrimage route across Britain. In the USA a dramatic new pilgrimage route has been created focusing upon the atomic bomb and its development and test sites. Starting from Albuquerque and ending in Livermore, north of San Francisco, this pilgrimage is one of sorrow and repentance and a call for peace in the face of our destructive skills and inclinations.

Such routes, old and new, take pilgrims across vast tracts of land and through varied landscapes. Travelling them with your eyes open to the changes and possibilities is one way of experiencing open spaces.

HARDY PLANTS FOR URBAN SPACES

Urban spaces can present a number of problems for gardeners: school playgrounds can be exposed and wind-blown, while city squares can be overshadowed by surrounding buildings. And if the only gardening space available in your own home is a roof terrace or balcony, you may suffer problems with lack of adequate water and excessively dry conditions. Here are some suitable plants for each of these conditions:

WIND-TOLERANT Trees

HIMALAYAN BIRCH (*Betula utilis*)

A hardy, deciduous mountain tree of small to medium height, up to about 20 m (60 ft) tall. Native to the Himalayas, Nepal, Kashmir and Afghanistan it is increasingly planted in cities for its attractive spring catkins and ornamental bark (in some varieties the bark is startlingly white and peels in horizontal papery flakes).

MOUNTAIN ASH OR ROWAN (*Sorbus aucuparia*)

A deciduous mountain tree that grows to a height of 5 to 15 m (15 to 45 ft), it is native to Europe, Asia Minor and Siberia where it can sometimes be found on craggy outcrops tolerating very windy conditions. This tree and related species are widely planted in cities for their hardiness, tolerance of shade and dry soil. Many of the ornamental varieties that are available become laden with masses of small, attractive, berry-like red fruits in the autumn.

Shrubs and Hedges

BARBERRY (*Berberis* spp.)

A large group of dense, thorny shrubs, some evergreen, and mostly drought tolerant. Grown for attractive, sometimes profuse flowers, and for their yellow, red or black berries which often persist into winter. Some species are useful for hedging e.g. *B. darwinii*.

ELDER OR ELDERBERRY (*Sambucus nigra*)

A deciduous shrub or small tree of up to 10 m (30 ft) in height found throughout Eurasia and north Africa. In spring it is cloaked in scented white flowers that are grouped in large inflorescences. In summer these ripen to form masses of juicy black elderberries. A wide range of cultivated forms are commonly found in gardens.

EUROPEAN HORNBEAM (*Carpinus betulus*)

This shade-tolerant Eurasian species can grow into a hardy deciduous tree of small to medium height, but is commonly trimmed as hedging for gardens. Cultivated in many ornamental forms.

SHRUBBY CINQUEFOIL (*Potentilla fructicosa*)

A popular deciduous garden shrub up to about 1.5 m (4 ft) high, planted for its bright yellow or white flowers in spring and summer. A wide range of cultivated forms and natural varieties are commonly found in gardens. Several of the more popular varieties come from China and the Himalayas.

OLEASTER (*Elaeagnus angustifolia*)

A deciduous west Asian shrub to 7 m (21 ft) in height, bearing attractive willow-like leaves tinged with silvery scales. Its sweet, fragrant flowers are yellow within, and silvery on the outside. Its fruits are yellow-brown, covered in silvery scales.

Perennials

BRUNNERA (*Brunnera macrophylla*)

Purple or blue flowering perennial herb up to 50 cm (2 ft) tall, with large basal leaves that can be different colours in cultivated forms.

NEW ZEALAND FLAX (*Phormium tenax*)

Evergreen perennial agave with stiff red-margined sword-shaped basal leaves and an inflorescence up to 5 m (15 ft) tall. Many cultivated forms are grown in gardens.

SPURGES (*Euphorbia* spp.)

A very large and diverse group, amongst which are several temperate perennial herbs with a range of flower colours. The Himalayan species *E. griffithi* grows 70 to 90 cm 2 to 3 ft) tall and bears pink-veined green leaves and copper or brick-red flowers.

YARROW (*Achillea* spp.)

A large group of perennial aromatic herbs about 60 cm to 1 m (2 to 3 ft) tall; some with fern-like leaves. Many species and garden forms. *A. millefolium* is typical, its garden forms bearing a range of flower colours from red to purple or pink to white.

Hardy Plants for Urban Spaces (cont.)

Annuals

ORACH (*Atriplex hortensis*)
An erect sun-loving Asian annual, up to 2.5 m (7 ft) tall.

PURPLE ORACH (*Atriplex hortensis* var. *rubra*)
This attractive naturally occurring variety of orach has purple-red or crimson triangular leaves and grows quickly, reaching a height of about 1 m (3 ft).

TOLERANT OF DRY CONDITIONS

Trees and Shrubs

BUTTERFLY BUSH (*Buddleja davidii*)
See page 139

CEANOTHUS (*Ceanothus* 'Delight')
Although many ceanothus are tender, this cultivar is hardy. The dense shrub grows to a height of 3 m (10 ft) and bears small blue to blue-purple flowers in late spring.

COTONEASTERS (*Cotoneaster sp.*)
Moderate to very hardy berry-bearing shrubs or small trees ranging from prostrate to bushy. May be deciduous or evergreen. Mostly planted for their conspicuous, often bright red, fruits. *C. horizontalis* is a commonly planted cotoneaster. It is a very hardy, low spreading shrub bearing bright orange-red fruit in late autumn.

FIELD MAPLE (*Acer campestre*)
A small shade-tolerant deciduous Eurasian tree or shrub to 12 m (36 ft) height, sometimes used for hedging. It is cultivated in many leaf forms and bears winged seeds in the autumn.

JAPANESE ROSE (*Rosa rugosa*)
This oriental rose grows 1–2 m (3 to 6 ft) tall with dense, prickly stems. It bears fragrant pink flowers in spring and red fruit in the autumn.

ROCK ROSE (*Cistus crispus*)
This low, wide, evergreen plant is frost resistant and hardy. Growing to a height of 60 cm (2 ft) in summer and almost twice as wide it features purple-red blooms in late summer.

ROSEMARY (*Rosmarinus officinalis*)
See page 45

RUE (*Ruta graveolens*)
An aromatic glaucous blue shrub, 20–50 cm (1 to 2 ft) tall, from southern Europe. Many garden forms in cultivation.

Perennials

BEAR'S BREECHES (*Acanthus mollis*)
A distinctive border plant from southern Europe and north Africa, growing up to 1 m (3 ft) in height, with toothed, spiny leaves and mauve or white flowers. Cultivated in several forms.

DYER'S CHAMOMILE (*Anthemis tinctoria*)
A yellow and white flowering perennial, growing up to 60 cm (2 ft) tall; from Europe, the Caucasus and Iran. Many cultivated forms available for the garden.

ICE PLANT (*Sedum spectabile* syn. *Hylotelephium spectabile*)
A succulent-leaved Chinese perennial; bearing nectar-rich, pale pink to dull red flowers, clustered in dense heads up to 70 cm (2 ft) tall. Many garden forms available.

ORIENTAL POPPY (*Papaver orientale*)
A popular Asian perennial, growing up to 90 cm (3 ft) tall, and bearing red, orange or pale pink flowers. Over seventy different cultivated forms are available.

CHURCHYARDS AND BURIAL GROUNDS

The church and its churchyard have long been an essential part of the European and indeed North American rural scene. The church building with its tower or spire and the churchyard with its jumble of lichen-encrusted headstones set amongst the rolling fields and nestling villages is the archetypal rural idyll. The history of the churches is usually well documented, as with most buildings, but the churchyards have been rather overlooked, though they have a fascinating history themselves. It is not for nothing that

SHADE-TOLERANT
Trees, Climbers and Shrubs

BARBERRY (*Berberis* spp.)
see page 149

CAMELLIA (*Camellia japonica* 'Alba Simplex')
A fairly hardy evergreen shrub, generally 2 to 3 m (6 to 9 ft) tall, but up to 9 m (27 ft) with age; flowering late winter or early in the spring. 'Alba Simplex' is a variety with single white flowers that is very resistant to weather.

COMMON BOX (*Buxus sempervirens*)
An evergreen native to Britain, box has been grown as a border for medieval herb beds and as the basis of an English knot garden. Unpruned box makes an elegant tree to 3 m (10 ft).

EVERGREEN EUONYMUS (*Euonymus japonicus*)
A shade-tolerant evergreen shrub from China and Japan with thick glossy leaves. It grows up to 8 m (24 ft) in height. Pink flowers. Many garden forms are available.

HONEYSUCKLE (*Lonicera pileata*)
This shrubby evergreen accepts dry shade under trees and grows to a height of 60 cm (2 ft) and about 1m to 1.5 m (4 to 5 ft) across. It features yellow-white fragrant flowers in summer followed by purple berries in autumn.

JUNIPER (*Juniperus communis*)
See page 107.

MEXICAN ORANGE BLOSSOM (*Choisya ternata*)
A shade tolerant evergreen Mexican shrub up to 2 m (6ft) tall; wide-spreading. It bears clusters of sweet-scented white flowers. Not wind tolerant but otherwise hardy.

Rosa 'New Dawn'
A rambler rose bred for cultivation in 1930 in the USA, 'New Dawn' holds the first plant patent ever granted. It is a 'big' climber for large spaces, growing 3 to 5 m (9 to 15 ft) tall, and bearing fragrant flowers that appear throughout the season. Bloom colour is a creamy-pink, fading to white during hot summer days. It is bred specifically for poor growing conditions, tolerating poor soil, partial shade, heat and cold.

YEW (*Taxus baccata*)
Evergreen Eurasian shrub or tree to 15 m (45 ft) in height with glossy, dark green leaves and red fruit-like arils (fleshy cones). Long cultivated; many garden forms are available.

Perennials

COMMON FOXGLOVE (*Digitalis purpurea*)
See page 122.

Epimedium × *rubrum*
This attractive ground cover features red blooms in late spring and grows to a height of 30 cm (12 in). The leaves turn orange and yellow in autumn.

HELLEBORE (*Helleborus* spp.)
A group of Eurasian shade-loving perennial herbs with large basal leaves. The Christmas rose *H. niger* has leathery, over-wintering, basal leaves and solitary white flowers (up to 30 cm (1 ft) tall) in winter or spring. Many garden forms of this and related species such as the Lenten rose *H. orientalis*, are available.

HOSTA (*Hosta fortunei*)
A low-growing, clump-forming, shade-loving Chinese herbaceous perennial with large leaves in a basal mound. Its flowers (up to 90 cm [3 ft]) are often violet and appear in the late summer. Many garden forms available.

LUNGWORT (*Pulmonaria* spp.)
A low-growing group of shade-loving Eurasian perennial herbs, generally with spotted basal leaves and blue flowers. *P. officinalis* has white-spotted leaves and purple or red flowers and is available in many garden forms. *P. saccharata* also has spotted leaves; its flowers being violet-red or white. It is also available in many garden forms.

they have been described as 'God's acre', a sacred space set aside for the community, the dead and for God.

Many of the oldest British, Irish and Brittany churchyards, normally those with circular boundary walls, very ancient yew trees (*Taxus baccata*) or pre-Christian burial mounds within them, were originally ancient pagan or Celtic sites of worship which were adapted as the new religion of Christianity spread. Therefore, in a number of cases the churchyard, as a site of worship or ritual, predates the church building, often by hundreds of years.

Once a site had become Christian, a boundary wall was usually set up to demarcate it from the surrounding area and it is this separation that has made churchyards the splendid places that they are today. Many churchyards were simply carved out of ancient pasture and meadowland and, owing to their boundaries, have escaped the ravishes of agricultural 'improvement', intensification and urban sprawl. In effect, therefore, what has survived in many rural areas as well as in some urban areas are small pockets of ancient semi-natural grassland. In the late 1980s and early 1990s the British Nature Conservancy Council, now English Nature, estimated that in the post-war period alone Britain had lost 98% of its semi-natural grassland, an extremely important habitat for grassland plants, and that a majority of the remaining 2% was held within the country's churchyards.

In an attempt to conserve this important natural resource the NCC, together with the Arthur Rank Centre, the British rural ecumenical centre in Warwickshire, England, established the Living Churchyard Project. Its aim is to help the managers of churchyards and burial grounds throughout the UK realise the importance of the land and manage it accordingly. This project has been very successful and, over the past decade, has helped over 5,000 churchyards to conserve their grassland. The idea has inspired similar initiatives and projects elsewhere in Europe and has contributed to the Environmental Audit programmes of North American churches.

The primary purpose of a churchyard or burial ground is, obviously, for the burial of the dead and, perhaps more importantly, to serve as a focal point where the deceased's friends and relations can quietly come to focus their grief. Over the past 30 years a strange, suburban notion has emerged that churchyards and cemeteries should be made to look 'neat'. This frantic suburbanisation of rural areas has left the countryside littered with thousands of churchyards that look like cricket pitches or bowling greens with headstones in them, providing they haven't been removed and made into a path or dumped underneath the boundary hedge! This has left them often almost completely devoid of any interest and, ironically for an age so obsessed with conserving its heritage, it is a complete break from traditional management. Churchyards in Europe and early colonial North America were originally used as hay meadows with the rights of herbage going to the vicar or minister. As such, the scene in early to midsummer would have been fabulous, for instead of serried ranks of cleaned headstones sitting on a lawn of rye grass there would have been a gently waving haze of different grasses dotted with ox-eye daisies, poppies, cornflowers and yellow rattle, and cowslips and primroses, together with wild daffodils in late spring, would

ABOVE: With creative planting, a cemetery can celebrate life and regeneration, as in this spectacular example in São Miguel in the Azores.

have lined the way into the church for the faithful – a celebration in reality of creation.

The idea that long grass is 'untidy' or that conservation is simply 'letting things go' is a widespread misconception and the Living Churchyard Project believes that conserving these potential havens for wildlife creates an atmosphere within the churchyards and cemeteries which is of benefit to grieving visitors. By encouraging wildlife such as butterflies, birds and plants into a churchyard the gloom is lifted and they cease to be places where the sorrow of death alone is remembered and also become sites for the celebration of the continuity of life.

Cemeteries

Cemeteries are a more recent development, springing up on the edges of towns and cities in order to cater for the rise in population. If one looks at a city churchyard, the ground to either side of the paths is often much higher, owing simply to the number of burials that have taken place there. The cemeteries served as an overflow facility to these original churchyards.

The great cemeteries, such as Highgate in London, the Glasgow Necropolis, Scotland, Eastern Suburbs, Bronte, Sydney, Australia, or Queens, New York, were designed by great landscape architects of the time, such as Paxton, and had two purposes. The functional one has already been mentioned but the second was to act as a public park, a place for the gentry of the period to stroll and socialise. As such, these places were created on a very large scale, often incorporating fantastic chapels and buildings, and were really some of the first arboretums. The Victorian cemeteries were reflections of the age of horticultural discovery, incorporating beautiful avenues and specimen trees, such as *Araucaria araucana*, the Chilean pine or monkey puzzle tree. Great monuments to civic leaders were erected, made from stone imported from all over the world, and many firms of masons made their reputations if they were asked to make a monument for a dignitary of the right status.

However, as cemetery design progressed, the skill of design which featured so highly in the original cemeteries was lost and harsh practicality took over. Modern cemeteries are designed with ease of maintenance in mind, incorporating headstones that can be sprayed with herbicide to keep them free of lichen or moss and which are set at a sufficient distance apart to run a gang mower between them. Unlike the First World War cemeteries in Normandy, with the simple white crosses on a green background, all identical yet speaking clearly of overwhelming loss and as a symbol of comradeship, these modern city cemeteries look lifeless and sterile.

In recent years, however, with the help of bodies like the Wildlife Trusts, English Nature and the Living Churchyard Project, cemeteries and churchyards are beginning to take on a new dimension, one of trying to welcome their visitors into a burial ground which is managed just as much for life as it is for death.

York Cemetery, England

The story of York cemetery, a large site just out of the city centre, was a sad one for many years, with a high level of vandalism and a lack of maintenance in many areas. This is, unfortunately, the case with many similar sites today. Under a new warden, however, the cemetery has turned from a depressing mess of bramble and rank grassland into a wonderful haven for both wildlife and people.

In working on such a large site it was easy to create sections of habitat, such as different grassland lengths, butterfly gardens and woodland. By taking biology down to its basics it was found that simply the provision of water in the cemetery attracted a large number of birds and mammals.

Certain areas of the cemetery were planted with wildflower seed and managed as a meadow. The grass in these sections is mown two or three times every year and the cuttings removed after the mowing. This means that the nutrient level in the soil is kept down to a minimum and therefore the less aggressive plants and grasses have a chance to thrive. This principle applies throughout all forms of wildlife gardening – native wildflowers prefer soil with a low fertility level. If the soil is too fertile, then rank grassland full of invasive species such as cow parsley and nettles will take over.

Cemeteries are seen as places for the dead, an idea that is stretched to the limit in countless horror movies. The cemetery is a place of foreboding, especially at night, though you are more likely to come across vandals than werewolves. Vandalism in cemeteries is a widespread problem.

In York they decided to tackle this problem head on and open up the cemetery so it ceased to become a forbidden place. Through their educational officer they got young people into the cemetery and one of the things they did was to create a butterfly garden. This was done by selecting a strip with a sunny aspect against a wall with little wind. This simulates the still woodland glades where you are most likely to find butterflies in the wild. They then planted flowering shrubs and plants such as viburnum, buddleia and lilac. This not only provided a sanctuary for insects such as butterflies and bees in the centre of the city but also considerably cut down on the incidence of vandalism, working on the principle that you are less likely to want to destroy something that you helped to create.

On a warm still day in midsummer, York cemetery is one of the most pleasant places in an already beautiful city.

This book has sought to take you on journeys into sacred gardens from the window box to New York's Central Park! We hope that we have made it possible for you to see the sacred potential in all that lies around you. The English 14th-century mystic Mother Julian of Norwich believed that an acorn contained the world. The Psalmists say that not even the Heavens can contain God. So it is with the sacred within all gardens.

APPENDIX 1: KEY TO MARIAN GARDEN

(see page 71)

1. **Rose arbour**
2. **Conifer** (*Cupressus macrocarpa* 'Gold Crest' or *Juniperus virginia* 'Burkii')
3. **Path**
4. **Border of pinks** (*Dianthus*) **and periwinkles** (*Vinca* spp)

A. Birth section
Shrubs:
A1 Dogwood (*Cornus alba*)
A2 *Berberis* 'Rubrostilla'
A3 *Viburnum carlesii* 'Diana'
Taller herbaceous plants:
A4 *Anemone x hybrida* 'Whirlwind'
A5 *Cimicifuga simplex*
Medium:
A6 Michaelmas daisy (*Aster laterifolius* 'Delight')
A7 *Ceratostigma plumbaginoides*
A8 *Vaccinuim angnolium*
A9 *Sternbergia*
Low:
A10 *Cyclamen hederifolium* var. *album*
A11 Snowdrop (*Leucojum autumnale*)
A12 Gentian (*Gentiana sino-ornata*)
A13 Crocus (*Crocus pulchella* 'Oxian')

B. Annunciation section
Taller:
B1 *Berberis x stenophylla*
B2 *Cystus* 'All Gold'
B3 *Japonica Acer*
Low (carpet of white and blue flowers):
B4 Barrenwort (*Epimedium x youngianum* 'Niveum')
B5 Dead nettle (*Lamium maculatum* 'White Nancy')
B6 Lily of the Valley (*Convallaria majalis*)
B7 Lungwort (*Pulmonaria* 'Sissinghurst Castle')
B8 Grape hyacinth (*Muscari* spp)
B9 Siberian scilla (*Scilla siberica*)
B10 Hyacinth (*Hyacinthus orientalis* 'Blue Magic')
B11 Bluebells *Hyacinthoides* spp)

C. Purification section
Taller:
C1 *Mahonia x media* 'Buckland'
C2 *M.* 'Charity'
C3 Christmas box (*Sarcocca hookeriana*)
C4 Witch hazel (*Hamamelis* spp)
C5 *Viburnum x bodnantense* 'Dawn'
C6 Dogwood (*Cornus alba* 'Aurea')
Medium:
C7 *Skimmia japonica* 'Rubella'

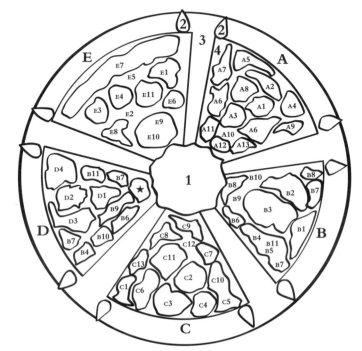

Low:
C8 Ground ivy (*Glechoma hederacea*)
C9 Variegated English ivy (*Hedera helix* 'Glacier')
C10 Japanese spindle (*Euonyymus fortunei* 'Variegatus')
C11 Variegated periwinkle (*Vinca minor* 'Argentomarginata')
C12 Christmas rose (*Helleborus niger*)
C13 Snowdrops (*Galanthus nivalis*)
C14 Winter aconite (*Eranthus hymenalis*)

D. Passion section
Tall:
D1 *Camellia japonica* 'Fred Sander'
D2 Japanese maple (*Acer palmatum*)
D3 *Rhododendron* 'Humming Bird'
D4 Narcissi
Low:
★ See Annunciation section

E. Assumption section
Tall:
E1 *Iris germanica*
E2 *Iris* 'Florentina'
E3 *Lilium candidum*
E4 *Paeonia officinalis*
E5 Shasta daisy (*Leucanthemum x superbum*)
D6 Feverfew (*Tanacetum parthenium*)
D7 Rose (*Rosa* 'Iceberg' and 'White Pet')
Lower:
E8 *Hebe albicans*
E9 *G.* 'Kashmir White'
E10 *Geranium wallichianum* 'Buxton's Blue'
E11 *Hellebore*

OTHER SUITABLE PLANTS INCLUDE:
Annunciation section
Crocus 'Bowle's White'
Glory of the snow (*Chinodoxa forbesii* 'Alba')
Viola odorata
Purification section
Silver blackberry (*Rubus cockburnianus*)
Willow (*Salix daphnoides*)
Heather (*Erica x darlyensis* 'White Perfection')
White pansy (*Viola* 'White Perfection')
Snowflakes (*Leucojum vernum*)
Cyclamen cuom.
Assumption section
P. mascula subsp. *arietina*
Potentilla 'Farrier's White'
Cystus x corbariensis
Geranium renardii
Asperula odorata
Campanula allianifolia
Veronica gentianoides
Salvia patens
Red hot poker (*Knifophia*)
Anchusa
Rudbeckia
Tagetes
Coreopsis

APPENDIX 2: SACRED GARDENS AROUND THE WORLD

Christian Gardens

Gethsemane Gardens – Christchurch, New Zealand
A classical romantic garden design with a Christian theme running through it.

Warsaw Biblical Gardens – Warsaw, Indiana, USA
Established in 1985 these biblically themed gardens cover a four acre site.

Lucile Halsell Conservatory – San Antonia, Texas, USA
Includes a biblical and sensory garden as well as wildflower and children's gardens. Covers 33 acres.

The Cloister Garden – Lincoln Cathedral, Lincoln, England
Incorporates a garden with plants dedicated to Our Lady. Although it is a very compact garden it is still very attractive, nestling in the centre of one of England's most beautiful cathedrals.

The Grotto, The National Sanctuary of our Sorrowful Mother – Portland, Oregon, USA
Includes a rose garden but perhaps the most stunning design is the Marguerite M. Casey Peace Garden which is essentially a sensory garden built along biblical themes.

Urban Gardens

The Path of Life Garden, St. Christopher's, Manchester, UK
This garden has been created on a housing estate. The heart of the garden design is a great natural rock surrounded by four gardens, one each for the four seasons, as well as for the four stages of life – childhood, youth, maturity and old age. A meandering path leads to the centre, representing the spiritual journey of life.

York Cemetery, York, England
A revitalised cemetery featuring wildflower meadows, butterfly gardens and woodland.

Bolton Percy Churchyard, Yorkshire, England
A small village churchyard featuring a flower garden amongst the gravestones.

Tealby Church, Lincolnshire, England
A small memorial garden featuring medieval plants and herbs.

Brooklyn Botanic Garden – Brooklyn, New York, USA
An impressive urban garden which is the centre for horticultural research in this area of the USA.

Kett Garden – Christchurch, New Zealand
This very compact garden shows what can be done with a small area of land in a typical urban setting.

Gardens for Reflection

Miyazu Japanese Garden – Nelson, New Zealand
A Japanese style garden which has been built for peaceful walks and personal reflection.

Dartington Hall, Devon, England
A garden featuring both naturalistic and abstract sculptures.

Tyler Rose Garden – Tyler, Texas, USA
A garden for reflection and peaceful meditation build as part of America's largest public rose collections. The centre also includes a collection of historic roses.

International Peace Garden – Boissevain, Manitoba, Canada
This enormous set of gardens straddles the border between Canada and the USA. It is affiliated to the National Park Service and includes wonderful floral bedding displays.

Sensory Gardens

Gertrude Jekyll's Garden, Munstead Wood, England
Probably the finest example of the great garden designer's work, this garden features lawns, shrubberies, rock gardens and woods.

Monet's Garden, Giverney, France
The garden which inspired some of Claude Monet's most famous paintings of water lilies.

Harmony Gardens – Coromandel Town, New Zealand
This relatively new garden was designed as a place of peace and tranquillity. It was built for walking, with vistas in mind and is a garden for all seasons.

Memphis Botanic Garden – Memphis, Tennessee, USA
The sensory garden is only one of 24 formal gardens within this 96 acre site in the mid-south USA.

Kirstenbosch National Botanical Garden – Cape Town, South Africa
Possibly the most impressive and comprehensive botanic garden in South Africa, covering 528 hectares. It was founded in 1913 and features medicinal as well as sensory gardens.

Monastic Gardens

Gardens of the Cloisters, Fort Tryon Park, New York, USA
Secular cloisters planted with plants typical of medieval European gardens.

Queen Eleanor's Garden, Winchester Castle, Winchester, England
Recreation of a 13th century castle garden.

Michelham Priory, Hailsham, Sussex, England
Cloister garden and physic garden based on the 9th century St Gall Monastery in Switzerland.

The Shrewsbury Quest, Shropshire, England
Recreated monastic garden including a physic garden, vegetable garden, turf garden and green court.

Abbaye Royale de Fontevraud, Fontevraud, France
Recreated monastic garden.

Sir Roger Vaughan's Garden, Tretower Court, Crickhowell, Powys, Wales
Recreation of a 15th century courtier's garden.

Islamic Gardens

Yves Saint Laurent's Garden, Marrakesh, Morocco
This garden was recreated at a recent Chelsea Flower Show in London.

Global Garden, Burgess Park, Southwark, England
This garden features a range of types of garden from around the world, including an Islamic-style courtyard.

The Garden of Heart's Delight, Shiraz, Iran
A classic Persian garden.

Garden of the Azem Palace, Damascus
Created in 1749 this garden in the heart of the souq of the old city, features a pond, arbours and hedges.

Tomb of Humayan, Delhi, India
An early Mogul garden.

Taj Mahal, Agra, India
Sacred geometry is embodied in the relationship between the mausoleum and the gardens.

Nishat Bagh, Lake Dal, Kashmir
An elaborate Mogul garden arranged on 12 terraces, one for each sign of the Zodiac.

Alhambra Palace, Granada, Spain
Built by the Moors in the 14th century.

Chinese Taoist Gardens

Palace Garden of Peaceful Longevity, Summer Palace, Beijing, China

Chengde garden, Hebei
The largest formal park and garden in China, these were the formal Imperial Summer Retreat of the Qing court, begun in 1703.

Chinese Garden, Darling Harbour, Sydney, Australia
A gift from the people of China to mark Australia's bicentennial of settlement, this garden features moon gates, temples, a rock garden and tea house.

Nanjing, Jiangsu – Zhan Yuan and Mochou Lake
These two gardens date from the Ming period, although they have been through many changes since that time.

Da Ming Lake, Jinan, Shandong
Once fed by seventy-two springs, the over-use of water has run most of these dry. Nevertheless this is a beautiful lake garden.

Suzhou, Jiangsu
There are many beautiful gardens here such as Lin Yuan and Hsi Yuan, all focussed around the famous waterways and lakes in the region. Essentially Suzhou is a city of gardens.

Jichang Yuan, Wuxi, Jiangsu
Spectacular walled gardens of the Ming period (1368 – 1644) situated in Xihui Park.

Hua Qing Lake hot spring gardens, Xian, Shaanxi
Situated about twenty kilometers outside Xian.

Japanese Gardens

Saiho-ji Buddhist Temple, Kyoto, Japan
One of the most famous of all moss gardens is the Saiho-ji in Kyoto. This is housed in the grounds of the Saiho-ji Buddhist Temple, also known as the Moss Temple. So popular is this garden that you have to book a slot to visit weeks beforehand. Before you are allowed into the garden you spend an hour or two chanting sutras to prepare yourself spiritually for the visit.

Hakone Art Museum
On a smaller scale to Saiho-ji is the moss garden in the grounds of the Hakone Art Museum, the former home of a founder of a new Shinto movement in the 1930s. Here Shinto reverence for the kami combined with an almost pure aesthetics has created a space of immense beauty and peacefulness.

MOA Museum, Atami, Japan
A tea house garden in the grounds below the museum.

Ryoan-ji, Kyoto, Japan
One of the most famous Zen gardens in the world, it is 500 years old and features 15 rocks placed in groups on a raked gravel bed.

Yosui-en, Wakayama, Japan
A stroll garden recreating a famous view of the Western Lake of Hangzhou, China.

Huntingdon Botanic Gardens, San Marino, California, USA
A Zen garden is contained within a larger Japanese-style garden.

University of Warwick, Coventry, England
This Zen garden is based on the parable of the ox and the herdsman, an allegory for the growth of enlightenment.

St Mungo Museum, Glasgow, Scotland
This Zen garden was created by Yasutaro Tanaka, a leading Japanese Zen garden designer from Kyoto.

Daisen-in, Kyoto, Japan
This Zen garden is found within the Daitoku-ji monastery and uses gravel, sand and rock to represent a waterfall.

GENERAL INDEX

Entries in *italics* denote illustrations

PLANT INDEX